PHILIP'S *Red Books showing*

LOCAL STREET ATLAS

C000051192

NEW FOREST

BEAULIEU · BROCKENHURST · CHRISTCHURCH · FORDINGBRIDGE
LYMINGTON · MILFORD ON SEA · RINGWOOD

CONTENTS

Page Layout & Road Map................. 2-3
2½ Miles to 1 Inch

Street Maps.................................... 4-27
4 Inches to 1 Mile

Index to Streets................................28

www.philips-maps.co.uk

First published in 2003 by
Estate Publications

This edition published by Philip's,
a division of Octopus Publishing Group Ltd
www.octopusbooks.co.uk
2–4 Heron Quays, London E14 4JP
An Hachette Livre UK Company

Third impression 2009
06/09-03

ISBN 978-0-540-09356-4

© Philip's 2008

This product includes mapping data licensed
from Ordnance Survey®, with the permission
of the Controller of Her Majesty's Stationery
Office.© Crown copyright 2003. All rights
reserved. Licence number 100011710

Printed in China by Toppan

Symbol	Description
	Minor Road
	Pedestrianized / Restricted Access
	Track
	Built Up Area
	Footpath
	Stream
	River
	Canal
	Railway / Station
●	Post Office
P	Car Park / Park & Ride
C	Public Convenience
+	Place of Worship
→	One-way Street
i	Tourist Information Centre
▲ ▲	Adjoining Pages
	Area Depicting Enlarged Centre
	Emergency Services
	Industrial Buildings
	Leisure Buildings
	Education Buildings
	Hotels etc.
	Retail Buildings
	General Buildings
	Woodland
	Orchard
	Recreational / Parkland
	Cemetery

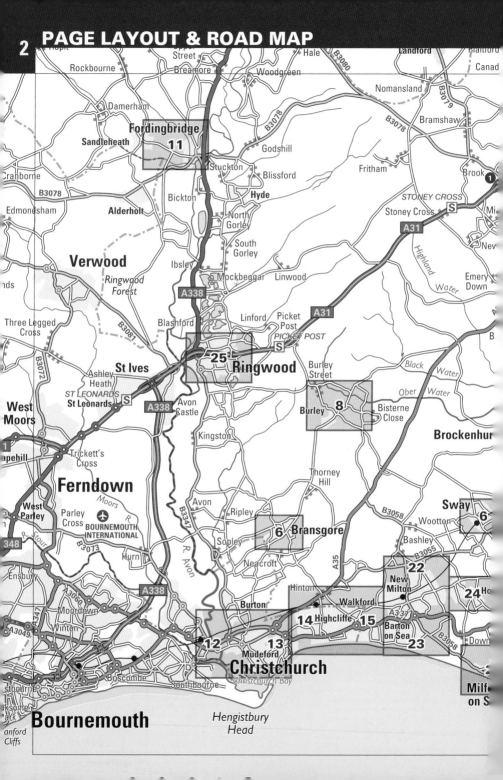

A36
A3090
Lee
ST WELLOW
S
M3
14
Fai
Oak
Horton
Heath
ROWNHAMS
S
Upton
Rownhams
SOUTHAMPTON
Ower
2
M27
A36
Nursling
3
Bassett
West
End
bridge
Calmore
A36
A35
Portswood
Swaythling
M27
A27
Dur
Long
Comm
Copythorne
A336
Totton
SOUTHAMPTON
Bitterne
Hedge
End
Botl
Cadnam
26
27
Shirley
Notham
Thornhill
9
A336
Netley
Marsh
A326
A35
Eling
Millbrook
A3025
Sholing
7
Woolston
R. Hamble
Burridge
A3024
8
Woodlands
Pooksgreen
Bursledon
B3397
A337
4
Marchwood
Netley
Lower
Swanwick
A27
Ashurst
Sarisbury
Hythe
Hamble-
le-Rice
Lock
Heat
ndhurst
16
17
SOUTHAMPTON WATER
Dibden
Purlieu
Warsash
B3056
B3054
A326
Hardley
Balmerlawn
Holbury
Fawley
Hill
Top
Beaulieu
5
Blackfield
10
B3053
B3055
Lymington River
Setley
Beaulieu
Heath
B3054
Langley
Calshot
East
Boldre
Bucklers
Hard
Exbury
Boldre
Beaulieu R.
nsley
Norleywood
Lepe
Stansore
Pt.
Portmore
East End
Cowes
Needs Ore
Pt.
East
18
19
Gurnard
R. Medina
A3020
A3021
Everton
Lymington
The
Solent
Lymore
Lower
Pennington
Thorness
Bay
Northwood
Keyhaven
Newtown Bay
Porchfield
Parkhurst
A337
Hamstead
Parkhurst
Forest
Yarmouth
Cranmore
Newtown
A3054
Newport
Norton
Shalfleet
Thorley
A3054
Ningwood
Colwell Bay
Norton
Green
Wellow
Newbridge
B3401
Carisbrooke
Totland
B3401

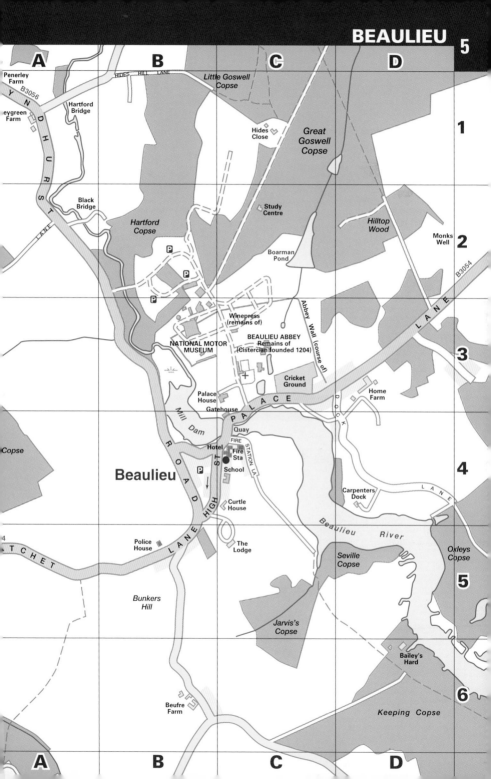

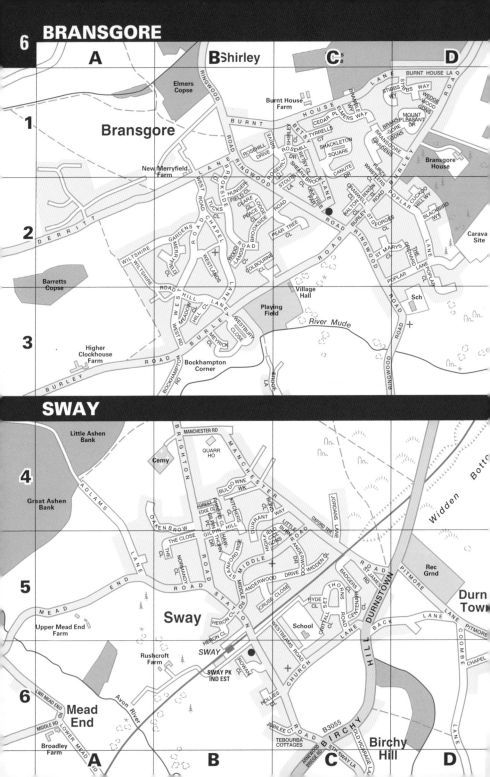

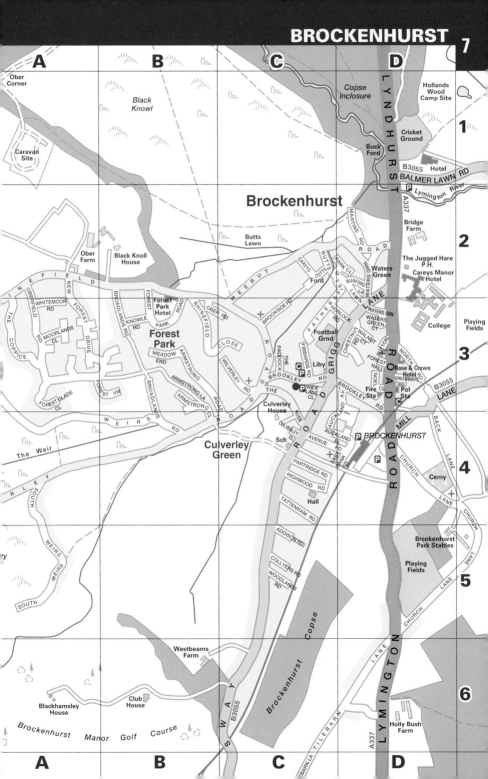

Brockenhurst

A — Ober Corner, Caravan Site, Ober Farm, THE COPPICE, OBERFIELD RD, MOORLANDS RD, MOORLANDS CL, FOREST GLADE CL, FOREST VW, FOREST DRIVE

B — Black Knowl, Black Knoll House, WHITEMOOR RD, KNOWLE RD, BROADLANDS RD, Forest Park, MEADOW END, ARMSTRONG LA, ARMSTRONG CL, NEW FOREST ROAD, RHINEFIELD CLOSE, WILVERLEY RD, Culverley House, Culverley Green, Blackhamsley House, Club House, Brockenhurst Manor Golf Course, Westbeams Farm

C — Copse Inclosure, Buck Ford, Brockenhurst, Butts Lawn, Forest Park Hotel, OBER RD, BROOKSIDE RD, MARTINS RD, BUTTS LAWN, CAREYS, COTTS, PARK CL, BURFORD CL, Waters Green, Ford, THE PADDOCK, THE BROOKLEY, FIBBARDS RD, Football Grnd, Liby, SHERLOCK RD, CHESTNUT RD, WALNUT CT, FOREST HALL, Fire Sta, GRIGG LANE, BROOKLEY RD, THE RISE, CULVERLEY CL, Sch, BANK RD, Brockenhurst, AUCKLAND AV, AUCKLAND RD, AVENUE, PARTRIDGE RD, HIGHWOOD RD, Hall, TATTENHAM RD, ADDISON RD, COLLYERS RD, WOODLANDS RD, Brockenhurst Copse, WAYS, B3055, TILEBARN LA, EBARN LA

D — Hollands Wood Camp Site, Cricket Ground, LYNDHURST RD, B3055, Hotel, BALMER LAWN RD, Lymington River, A337, Bridge Farm, The Jugged Hare P.H., Careys Manor Hotel, College, Playing Fields, NORTH RD, SUTTON RD, Rose & Crown Hotel, GREENWAYS RD, Pol Sta, B3055, MILL LANE, BACK LANE, CHURCH LANE, Cemy, Brockenhurst Park Stables, Playing Fields, LYMINGTON RD, A337, Holly Bush Farm

1, 2, 3, 4, 5, 6

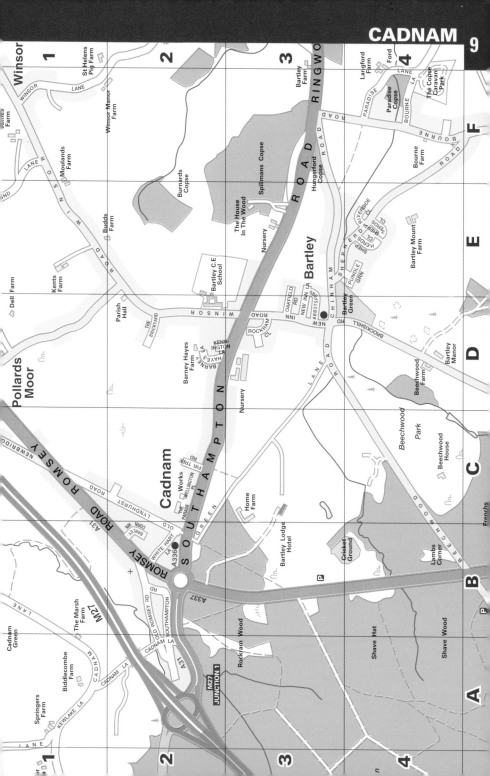

Map labels

10 FAWLEY

A B C D

1

Flare Stack
Flare Stack

SEVENTH ST
SEVENTH ST
FOURTH STREET
THIRD STREET
THIRD STREET
FOURTH AVENUE
AVENUE
AVENUE
FIRST STREET
FIRST STREET
SECOND STREET
MARSH LA
MARSH LANE
SALTERNS LA
RYE PADDOCK LA
LANE
CHURCHFIELD
COPTHORNE
COPTHORNE
ASHLETT
STONEHILL RO
B30

CHURCH LA
CHURCH LA
FOREST EDGE
ORCHARD CL
WOODVILLE RD
COLEVILLE RD
MEAD
THE AV
PADDOCKS
LINDA RD
THE SHERR
COPTHORNE
ADMIRALS WK
ASHLETT CL

2

OIL REFINERY

Kennels Row
SOUTH
FAWLEY ROAD
33053

Recreation Ground

Gang Warily Recreation Centre

ASHDOWN
School
FAWLEY
DENNY
CHARLES LEY CT
THE FALCON
THE LARGE LA
JESSOP
HALL MWS

Library
Hall

Fawley

BY PASS

3

The Fowey
PRIESTCROFT CL
THE HARLEY
HAYES MEAD
schools
WILVERLEY PL
X PENDLE
HUGHES GDNS
PENLETON GDNS

ASHDOWN RD
BLACKFIELD RD
CHAPEL LA
SLADES HILL
THE PENTAGON

DUN-FIELD COPSE
TOOMER CL
THORNHILL RD
MILLIKEN
RO SMITH

The Pentagon

FRY CL
BEVIS CL
SHELLEY CL
KEATS CL

HEATHER RD
FORESTERS RD
FURZEY CL
HEATHER CL
HEDLEY
DARK LANE

Fields Farm

4

Club
STAR
BATES
HARTS CL

BLACKFIELD ROAD
HAMPTON LANE
NEW ROAD
GROVE CL
HARTSGROVE AV
ST MICHAELS
EDWARD CL
NEWLANDS
NEWLANDS CL
NEWLANDS COPSE
WALKERS COPSE

Fields Heath

5

Whitehaven Caravan Park
infield opse
my
JANES CL
HAMPTON GDNS
HAMPTON CL
NORTHAMPTON
HOLLY RD
THORNBURY
GEORGE ST
MOPLEY AV
WHEELERS WK
NORMAN RD
WESSEX CL
CEDRIC CL
VIKING RD
SAXON RD
NORTH CL

Queen Elizabeth II Recreation Ground

Toms Down

Tom's Down

Mopley Pond

Badminston Common

Badminston Plantation

6

CHAPEL LA
THE GLADE
EPE RD
BOWLAND
SMITH CL
CHALEWOOD RD
BERNWOOD
KINGS RD
BIRCHWOOD DR
WEST RIDE
ST FRANCIS RD
FOXY RD
COMMON CL
LINGLEY
LODGE GDNS
CLARE GDNS
FOXPOOL GDNS
DUCK CL
KEYES CL
FORGE RD
NICHOLAS RD
MOPLEY CL
WALKERS LANE
SOUTH LANE
GREEN LANE
FOREST GATE
LA GLADE
EPE ROAD
LEP

Dean's Bridge

Newhouse Copse

A B C D

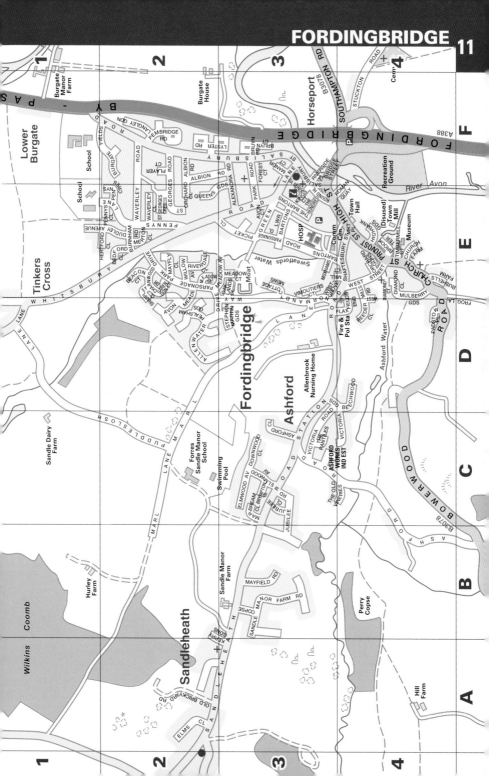

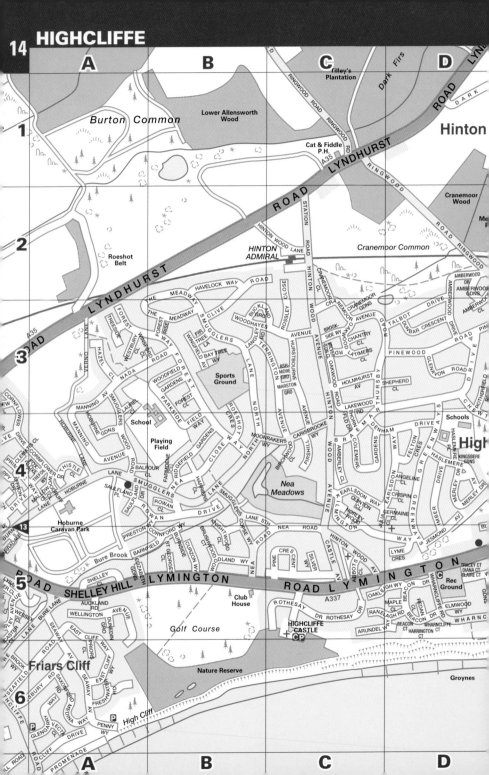

A B C D

1

Burton Common

Lower Allensworth Wood

Trilley's Plantation

Dark Firs

RINGWOOD ROAD

RINGWOOD RD

Cat & Fiddle P.H.
A35

LYNDHURST ROAD

Hinton

2

Roeshot Belt

LYNDHURST ROAD

HINTON WOOD LANE

HINTON ADMIRAL

STATION ROAD

HINTON WOOD

Cranemoor Common

RINGWOOD ROAD

Cranemoor Wood

Me R

AMBERWOOD DR
AMBERWOOD GDNS
AMBERWOO

3

A35 ROAD LYNDHURST

VERNON LANE
THREESIDE
FOREST LANE
HAZEL CL
NADA

WESTBURY
WINSFORD ROAD
FOREST WAY

THE MEADWAY
THE MEADWAY
THE FOREST RISE

HAVELOCK WAY ROAD
SMUGGLERS LA
CLIVE
WOODHAYES
FIR TREE LA
WINGFIELD RD
BAY TREE WY

BUCKLAND GRO
LANGLETERRINGTON
ROSSLEY CL
CLOSE

HURSTBOURNE AV
ASHMORE GRO
MARSTON GRO

CRANEMOOR AV
BROOKSIDE WY
CHANTRY CL
LATIMERS CL
OAKWOOD RD

CRANEMOOR GDNS

TALBOT ROAD
DUNBAR CRESCENT
PINEWOOD

DRIVE

Sports Ground

WOODFIELD
GARDENS
FOREST
PARKSIDE
FIELD WAY

ROESHOT CRES WAY
LANE NORTH

HINTON WOOD ROAD
AVENUE
CARISBROOKE WY

HOLMHURST AV
LAKEWOOD
THORNE FIELD

SHEPHERD CL

GLENAVON ROAD

CHEWT

School
Playing Field

MANNING AV
HOBURNE
SMUGGLERS
LAUREL
WOOD
GDNS

BALFOUR GL
FARMDENE
GEFIELD GARDENS

NEA RD
HARPERS LANE

MOONRAKERS WY
BIRCHWOOD AVENUE
FIRSHILL
THISHILL

AMBERLEY GRO
COLEMERE

THURSBY RD
FELTON CL

GARDENS
DENHAM

EARLSDON WAY

GREENWAYS
HASLEMERE

Schools

High

KINGSBERE GDNS

4

CORNFLOWER DRIVE
CLEMA
TREFOIL CL
THISTLE CL
WOODRUFF
MALLOW
FOX
PRIM
ARROW
POPPY
BRAMBLE

HOBURNE
MANNING LANE
AVENUE
WOOD ROAD

SAULFLAND PL
SAULFLAND LANE
ROWAN CL
ROWAN

SMUGGLERS LANE
SMUGGLERS LANE STH
DRIVE

NIGHTWOOD CL
BRUSHWOOD

NEA ROAD

QUINTON
NORLEY WOOD
GERMAINE CL
CRISPIN CL
ANGELINE CL

MERLEY DR
MERLEY AV

13

Hoburne Caravan Park

Bure Brook
PRESTON WY
CORNFORD WY
BARNFIELD
ST GEORGES
BURNSIDE
CURZON RD
ODLAND WY
NEA

PINE CRESCENT
SILVER WY

HINTON CASTLE AV

ABBOTS CL
LYME CRES

JESMOND

Nea Meadows

NEA ROAD

WHARNCLIFFE RD

5

SHELLEY HILL LYMINGTON ROAD

SHELLEY RD
AUCKLAND RD
WELLINGTON AV
ELIZABETH
BARNFIELD
DUNEDIN
AVENUE

LYMINGTON ROAD

A337

ROTHESAY DR
ROTHESAY DR

OAKLEIGH WY
RANELAGH RD
BEACON DR
REDAN DR
MAPLE CL

TRACEY CT
DIANA CT
BLAIRE CT

Rec Ground

ELMWOOD WY
WHARNCLIFFE RD
HARRINGTON CT
WHARNCL

Club House

HIGHCLIFFE CASTLE
CP

ARUNDEL WY
BEACON DR

Friars Cliff

Golf Course

6

SEAFIELD
CORNFLOWER
AYSABURY RD
SAXONFORD RD
MEDINA WY
EAST CLIFF
SEAWAY
PRIORS
CLIFF WAY
EAST CLIFF
SEAWAY AV

Nature Reserve

Groynes

HIGHCLIFFE
ROCLIFF ROAD
GLENGY CT
AVE VECTIS
PENNY WY

High Cliff

PROMENADE

A B C D

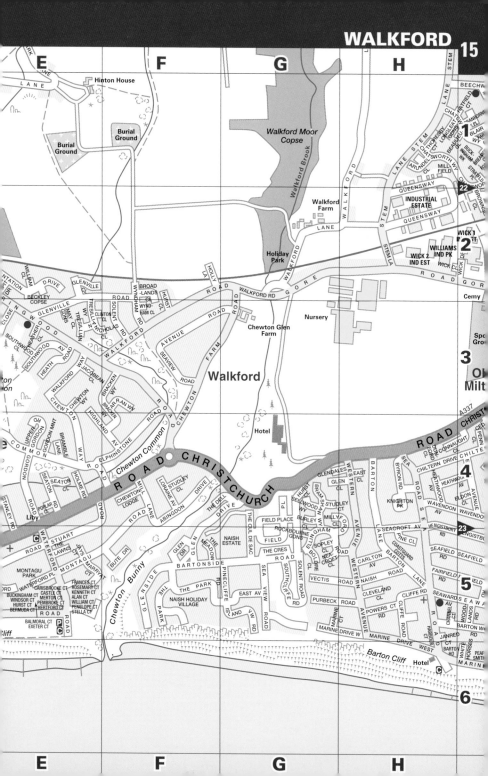

A   B   C   D

1

SWAY ROAD

Wheel Inn

Bowling Green

Didgemere Nursery

INDUSTRIAL PARK

BOWLING GRN RD

Buckland Rings

RAVENS-CROFT RD

Tollhouse Inn

Buckland

SOUTHAMPTON

A337

2

Little Ramley Farm

Lymington

RAMLEY ROAD

STRATFORD PL

PADDOCK GDNS

GROSVENOR

ALEXANDRA

BRAMBLE WY

REDWOOD CL

WOODLE

PARK RD

FILTON

KINGS

CRESSINGS

HOSP

ELIZABETH

HOWLETT CL

PAMPLYN CL

SAMBER CL

FULLERTON

3

Cowley Farm

Pinetops Nurseries

PINETOPS CL

NORTHOVER RD

BROWNINGS

YALDHURST MEAD

ST MARKS RD

Recreation Ground

COWLEY

DOWLANDS

HIGHFIELD

LINDEN WY

BERESFORD

BAYS RD

Cemetery

GREENWAY

LEIGH PARK CL

HIGHFIELD AV

WESTERN

MIDDLE

Super

Upper Pennington Common

UPPER COMMON RD

HAZEL ROAD

MIDDLE ROAD

COMMON

Upper Pennington

RAMLEY ROAD

LODGE EDWARDS LANE

BAYS RD

GORDON RD

WHITAKER CRES

GREENWAY

AVON CL

SOUTHERN

QUEEN

ROME

HILLSIDE

ST ANNES CL

GDNS

BRIESLANDS

4

Wainsford Bridge

WAINSFORD ROAD

WAINSFORD

Pennington Common

War Memorial

LAWN RD

CHEQUERS CL

GORDON RD

OLIVER

RENOUF

KERRY

PRIESTLANDS

ROAD

Schools

Pennington

NORTH

SOUTH

Leisure Centre

BROOKLAND CL

The Gurney Dixon Centre

Pennington Cross

5

Upper Rough

WAINSFORD ROAD

WEST PENNINGTON CL

BROOMHILL CL

EFFORD

NIBBORD CL

CORBIN

CONIFER CL

HOLMSLEY CL

WILVERLEY CL

EFFORD

JUNIPER

HOWARDS MEAD ROAD

WAINS MEAD

POUND ROAD

HAGLANE

LITTLE DENE COPSE

MEAD ROAD

MEADOW RD

WIDBURY ROAD

SOUTHLANDS

PENNINGTON FORWARD DR

WEST WAY

SLOE CL

GREENLANDS

NORTH

STREET

ELM CL

FOX POND

LEE-LANDS

KINGS PK

GRAFTON GDNS

MILFORD ROAD

RIVAUX

LOWER PENNINGTON LANE

Vineyard

Newlease Copse

Efford House

BROADLY CL

DENESIDE

HAGLANE COPSE

HAY-FORD

CLAUSEN WY

NEWBRIDGE

LONG

AV

6

Efford Farm House

MILFORD ROAD

A337

A337

A   B   C   D

E   F   G   H

1

2

3

4

5

6

Walhampton

School
Home Farm
Monument
Sandwalk Pond

Walhampton Wood

Monument

Lower Buckland

School

Toll

Monument

TOWN

I.O.W. Ferry
PIER
Marina

Ferry Terminal
Vehicle Ferry

Elmers Court

Rec Grnd
Horn Reach

Sea Water Baths
Royal Lymington Yacht Club

Waterford

Marina

Woodside Gardens
De La Warr House

Woodside

Playing Field

Normandy Farm

Normandy

HOSPITAL
D.C. Offices
T.H.
Comm Centre
Medical Centre
Fire Sta
Sports Ground
Bus Station
Liby
Schs
Mus

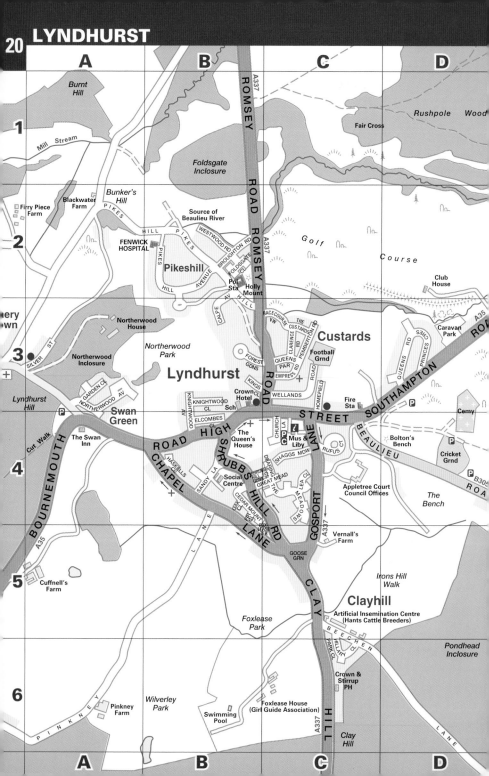

Lymore

Cox's Bridge

Fish Pond

Hotel

Barnes Farm

Nursery

Blackbush Copse

Shorefield Caravan Park

Holiday Park

Hordle Bridge

Downton

Sea Breeze Caravan Site

Shorefield Holiday Park

WARREN PARK

Shorefield Copse

Studland Common

Danes Stream

THE BUCKLERS

WEST

Hordle Manor Farm

Hordle House School

Playing Field

Hordle Cliff

Rock Cliff

St Georges Hospital

Recreation Ground

Pleasure Grounds

Milford Trading Est

Hospital

The White House

Caravan Park

Sturt Pond

Groynes

Milford on Sea

LYMINGTON ROAD

BARNES LANE

CLIFF ROAD

HURST ROAD

SEA ROAD

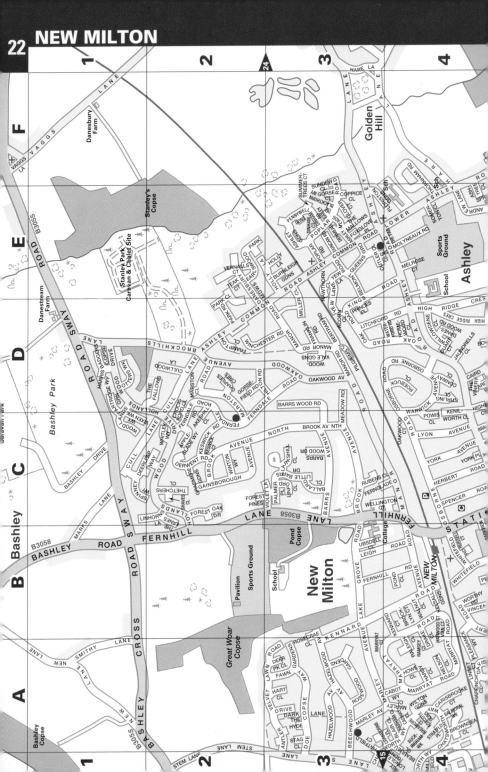

1 **2** **3** **4**

F

Danesbury Farm

VAGGS LA

Golden Hill

HARE LA

SUMMER TREES CT

E

ROAD B3055

Stanley's Copse

Stanley Park Caravan & Chalet Site

Danestream Farm

Sch

Sports Ground

Ashley

School

MELROSE

MOLYNEUX RD

HIGH RIDGE CRES

D

Bashley Park

BASHLEY ROAD SWAY LANE

BROCKHILLS

Winchester Rd

Manor Rd

OAKWOOD

BARRS WOOD RD

OAKWOOD RD

OSBORNE RD

C

Bashley

Bashley Copse

CULL ROAD

BROOK AVENUE

NORTH AVENUE

BROOK AV NTH

FERNDALE

FERNHILL LANE B3058

B

B3058

BASHLEY ROAD FERNHILL

Sports Ground

Pavilion

School

Pond Copse

New Milton

NEW MILTON STATION

WHITEFIELD

A

NEW LANE SMITHY LANE

B3055 BASHLEY CROSS ROAD

Great Wbar Copse

KENNARD AVENUE

MARRYAT ROAD

CARISBROOKE

1 **2** **3** **4**

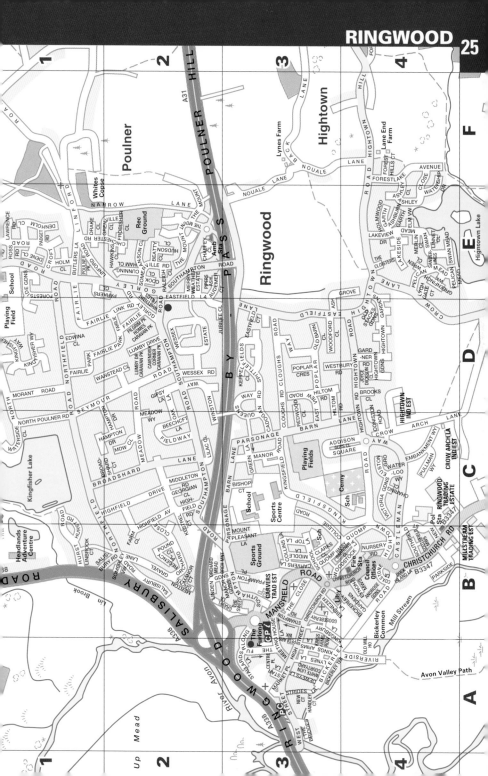

A
B
C
D
1
2
3
4
5
6
Shorn Hill
Calmore Village Hall
Little Testwood Farm
Bog Plantation
Broad Oak Farm
Calmore
Little Fir Clump
Tatchbury Mount Hospital
Recreation Ground
Griffin Industrial Park
Lulworth Business Park
South Hampshire Industrial Park
Totton Calmore Junior & Infants Schools
Recreation Ground
Hazel Farm
Superstore
Hammonds Green
Totton College
Recreation Centre
Hanger Farm
Upper Hanger Farm
Abbotswood School
Sch
Comm Centre
Health Centre
Netley Marsh
Thornlands Farm
Ashurst Bridge
Willswood Farm
Little Fletchwood Farm
Rushington Business Park
New Forest Enterprise Centre
TOTTON WESTERN BY-PASS
SALISBURY ROAD
RINGWOOD ROAD
CALMORE ROAD
HAMMONDS WAY
BLACKWATER DRIVE
LOPERWOOD LANE
COOKS LANE
PAULETTS LANE
ASHURST BRIDGE ROAD
FLETCHWOOD ROAD
FLETCHWOOD LANE
MICHIGAN WAY
STANLEY ROAD
SUTTON ROAD
TESTWOOD AV
STEPHENSON ROAD
EDDYSTONE RD
BRUNEL ROAD
NUTSEY AV
NUTSEY LA
NUTWOOD WAY
TENNYSON ROAD
SHELLEY RD
EWELL WAY
CALMORE DRIVE
CALMORE GARDENS
CALMORE CRES
ROWAN CL
DEERHURST CL
DORLAND GDNS
MONKTON LA
TESTBOURNE AV
TESTBOURNE CL
ABBOTTS WAY
BARNSFIELD CRES
BARNSFIELD CRESCENT
FRITHAM CL
RUFUS GDNS
MALWOOD GDNS
ASHBY RD
HAYWARD CL
ANDREW CL
COBLANDS AV
PLOVER DR
MAGPIE DR
HAZEL FARM RD
OAKDENE
WINCHESTER WAY
KINGSLEY GDNS
STRIDES WAY
CRABBS WAY
DICKENS DELL
PICKWICK CL
HUNTERS CRES
ROUNDHOUSE DR
SWALLOW CL
MAPLEWOOD CL
APPLEWOOD PL
LARCHWOOD AV
BRIARWOOD RD
EASTMEARE CT
COPINGER CL
ETHELRED GDNS
HAROLD CL
GRADIDGE WAY
SHERIDAN GDNS
BRONTE WAY
MEREDITH GDNS
MYRTLE AV
DRAYTON PL
LONGSTOCK CL
HEATHER CL
SALCOMBE RD
RUSHINGTON AV
DURLEY CRES
PENTRIDGE WAY
DENBIGH CL
MONMOUTH GDNS
IBBOTSON WAY
ROSELEIGH DR
HAMBERT WAY
ELLDENE CT
BARTLEY AV
TEDDER WAY
PORTAL RD
WINGATE DR
MONTGOMERY AV
MOUNTBATTEN RD
HARWOOD CL
ALEXANDER CL
BONIFACE CRES
BISHOPS CL
NORTHLANDS RD
HAWTHORNE GREEN
BRACKLEY WAY
KILNYARD CL
BLACKWATER MEWS
MORTIMER CL
ROTHBURY CL
CHARNWOOD CL
THE REDFORDS
SYLVIA CRES
CHEAM WY
HONEYWOOD CL
ALLERTON CL
SHRAVESHILL CL
BEARSLANE CL
AINTREE RD
FONTWELL CL
CORNFORTH RD
OATFIELD GDNS
TREAGORE RD
GREGORY GDNS
BOWATER WY
APPLETREE CL
MELROSE CT
THE SPINNEY
SILVERS WOOD
DAYRELL CL
SHEPHERDS RD
WOOD LODGE
THE DROVE
RICHMOND CL
CHARMUS RD
NUTSHALLING CL
AMBERWOOD CL
OLDBARN CL
WILDBURN CL
CROFT
FRIARS
SNELGROVE CL
STOCKLANDS
BUCKLAND GDNS
RANDALL CL
WARREN PL
COPPICE RD
BEECHDALE CL
THE CROFT
BIRCH CL
HERONS WOOD
EMBLEY CL
BENBOW GDNS
GLADE
THE PADDOCK
ARCHERS
CAMILLA CL
KATHRYN CL
AMEY WY
LAUREN WY
GARDENS
JESSICA CRES
GEORGINA CL
RUBY CL
CALIFORNIA CL
BARBERRY DR
OLEANDER DR
GARLAND WY
SINGLETON WY
RADLEIGH GDNS
SOVEREIGN CL
SLATER CL
TUDOR CL
CEDARWOOD
FLOWERDOWN CL
CHEPSTOW CL
WETHERBY GDNS
HAYDOCK
SEDGEFIELD
GOODWOOD GDNS
SANDLEWOOD CL
BUCKTHORN CL
SPRUCE DR
MANSERGH WK
ASPEN WK
STONECHAT DR
FIELDFARE CT
NIGHTINGALE DR
ROBIN GDNS
ALDER HILL DR
SHETLAND CL
CLYDESDALE WY
DALES WAY
EXMOOR CL
SHIRES WK
AIKMAN LA
CORIANDER DR
BULLFINCH CL
GOLDCREST CL
ALFRED CL
LOVAGE GDNS
MATLEY GDNS
OVIAT CL
SERLE CL
BURLEY CL
WELLERS CL
OLIVERS CL
COPPERFIELDS
HOLLAND WK
CYPRESS GDNS
A36
A336
A326

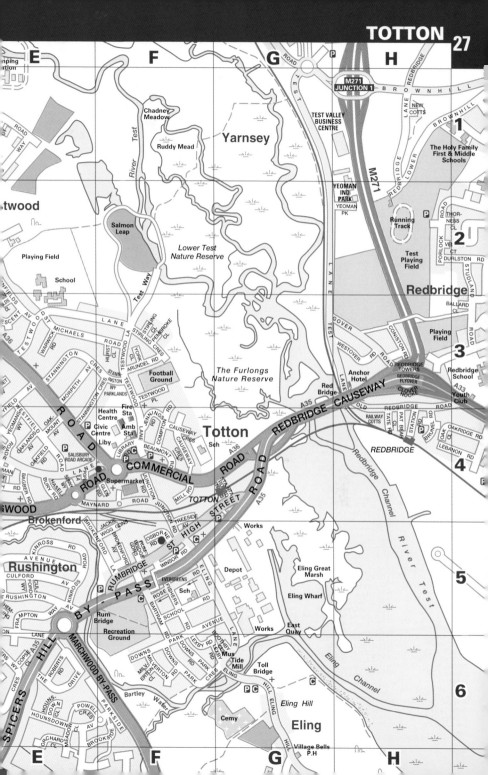

E F G H

M271 JUNCTION 1

BROWNHILL
LANE

NEW
COTTS

1

Chadney
Meadow

River Test

Ruddy Mead

Yarnsey

TEST VALLEY
BUSINESS
CENTRE

ROAD

REDBRIDGE LOWER

BROWNHILL

The Holy Family
First & Middle
Schools

twood

YEOMAN
IND
EST

YEOMAN
PK

M271

Running
Track

THORNESS
CL

PORLOCK

VEL
CT

DURLSTON RD

2

Salmon
Leap

Playing Field

School

*Lower Test
Nature Reserve*

Test Way

Test
Playing
Field

Redbridge

STUDLAND

BALLARD
CL

LANE

A36

TESTWOOD

WARWICK

MICHAELS

ROAD

HURST

STIRLING LA

STIRLING CRES

PEMBROKE
CL

YORK
RD

ARUNDEL RD

Football
Ground

TESTWOOD

PARKLANDS

*The Furlongs
Nature Reserve*

GOVER
ROAD

WESTOVER

CONISTON RD

LANE
TEST

Anchor
Hotel

Red
Bridge

REDBRIDGE
TOWERS

REDBRIDGE
FLYOVER

CLOVER
MOORE

OLD

Playing
Field

Redbridge
School

A33

Redbridge
Youth
Club

3

MORPETH

STANNINGTON
CRES

STANNINGTON
WY

TESTWOOD
PL

A35

REDBRIDGE CAUSEWAY

RAILWAY
COTTS

TATE RD

PAT BEAR

STATION

OAKRIDGE RD

LEBANON RD

BRUNEL RD

OAK

4

WESTFIELD
RD

YEOMANS
RD

OAK
MOUNT
AV

OAKLANDS
AV

OAKFIELD
RD

ROAD

LANE

SHIRLEY

Fire
Sta

Health
Centre

Civic
Centre

Liby

JENNINGS RD

COMPTON

Amb
Sta

CAUSEWAY
CRES

CAUSEWAY

Sch

Totton

A36

ROAD

ROAD

HIGH STREET

Redbridge Channel

REDBRIDGE

SALISBURY
ROAD ARCADE

Library

BEAUMONT
CL

CHADNEY
CL

COMMERCIAL

Supermarket

JUNCTION
ROAD

Mill Rd

TOTTON

A35

River Test

5

MAN

BAGBER
RD

BURY RD

SHIRLEY

LANE

GLEN
EYRE

MAYNARD

Brokenford

BROKENFORD
ROAD

WIGG GDNS

JACKIE

PURLIEU
GDNS

OSBORNE
RD

TREESIDE

JUNCTION RD

ST

Works

Depot

*Eling Great
Marsh*

Eling Wharf

Rushington

KINROSS
RD

AVENUE

CULFORD

KINROSS AV

RUSHINGTON

RUMBRIDGE

BY

PASS

WINDSOR RD

ELING

EVERGREENS

ROSE RD

FISHERS

Sch

Works

East
Quay

HAMPTON

FRAMPTON
WAY

LANE

Rum
Bridge

Recreation
Ground

BARTRAM

SCHOOL RD

AVENUE

Mus
Tide
Mill

Toll
Bridge

*Eling
Channel*

6

SPICERS HILL

THE
ROBERTS
RD

HOUNS
DOWN
CL

COPSE

CRES

MARCHWOOD BY-PASS

DRIVE

PARKSIDE

BROOKSIDE

POWELL
CRES

ORCHARD
MEADOW
CL

HOUNSDOWNS
CL

BARTLEY

DOWNS

MILVERTON

MILTON RD

ERTON

DOWNS
PARK

DOWNS
PARK
CRES

LEXBY RD

BROMLEY

LEXBY RD

ELING

Cemy

Eling Hill

HILL
ELING

Eling

Village Bells
P.H

E F G H

INDEX TO STREETS
with Postcodes

The Index includes some names for which there is insufficient space on the maps. These names are indicated by an * and are followed by the nearest adjoining thoroughfare.

A Avenue SO45 10 A1
Abbey Cl SO45 17 F3
Abbots Cl BH23 14 C5
Abbotsford SO40 9 D3
Abbottsfield SO40 26 D4
Abingdon Dr BH23 15 F4
Acacia Rd SO41 24 B1
Acorn Cl BH25 22 D3
Adams Rd SO45 17 F4
Addington Ct SO41 21 D2
Addington Pl BH23 12 D4
Addiscombe Rd BH23 12 A3
Addison Rd SO42 7 C5
Addison Sq BH24 25 C3
Adlams La SO41 6 A4
Admirals Cl SO45 10 D2
Admirals Way SO45 17 G2
Agarton La SO41 21 F1
Aikman La SO41 26 B4
Aintree Rd SO40 26 C2
Airfield Ind Est BH23 13 F4
Airfield Rd BH23 13 F3
Airfield Way BH23 13 F3
Airspeed Rd BH23 13 G3
Akeshill Cl BH25 22 C2
Alan Ct BH23 15 E5
Albany Cl BH25 23 B6
Albert Rd BH25 22 B4
Albion Rd SP6 11 F2
Aldbury Ct BH25 23 B8
Alder Cl, Christchurch BH23 12 C1
Alder Cl, Southampton SO45 16 C4
Alder Hill Dr SO40 26 B3
Alexander Cl, Christchurch BH23 13 E4
Alexander Cl, Southampton SO40 26 C4
Alexandra Cl SO45 17 F3
Alexandra Rd, Fordingbridge SP6 11 E3
Alexandra Rd, Lymington SO41 18 D2
Alexandra Rd, Southampton SO45 17 F2
Alfred Cl SO40 14 D4
All Saints Rd SO41 19 F5
Allenwater Dr SP6 11 D2
Allerton Cl SO40 26 C2
Ambassador Cl BH23 13 G4
Ambassador Ind Est BH23 13 F4
Amberley Cl BH23 14 D3
Amberley Ct SO40 26 D6
Amberslade Walk SO45 17 E5
Amberwood Cl, Christchurch BH23 14 D3
Amberwood Cl, Southampton SO40 26 B2
Amberwood Dr BH23 14 D2
Amberwood Gdns BH23 14 D2
Ambleside Rd SO41 19 F4
Ambury La BH23 13 E2
Amethyst Rd BH23 13 E3
Amsterdam Sq BH23 12 C4
Anchor Cl BH23 13 G6
Anchor Mws SO41 19 F3
Anchorage Way SO41 19 E4
Anderwood Dr SO41 6 B5
Andover Cl BH23 13 H3
Andrew Cl, Hythe SO45 17 F6
Andrew Cl, Southampton SO40 26 C4
Andrew La BH25 22 E4
Androse Gdns BH24 25 B4
Angel La BH25 23 E7
Angeline Cl BH23 14 D4
Anne Cl BH23 12 A1
Anson Cl, Christchurch BH23 13 F4

Anson Cl, Ringwood BH24 25 E2
Antler Dr BH25 22 A3
Appleslade Way BH25 22 C2
Appletree Cl, New Milton BH25 23 C6
Appletree Cl, Southampton SO40 26 B3
Applewood Pl SO40 26 B5
Archers Cl BH25 26 C2
Archgate SO41 19 E2
Arden Walk SO41 24 D4
Argyle Rd BH23 13 E6
Ariel Cl BH6 12 A6
Ariel Dr BH6 12 A6
Arlington Ct BH25 23 C7
Armada Dr SO45 17 E4
Armitage Av SO45 17 E6
Armstrong Cl SO42 7 B3
Armstrong La SO42 7 B3
Armstrong Rd SO42 7 B3
Arnolds Cl BH25 23 A7
Arnwood Av SO45 17 E6
Arran Way BH23 15 F3
Arthur La BH23 12 A3
Arthur Rd BH23 12 A3
Arundel Cl BH25 15 H1
Arundel Rd SO40 27 F3
Arundel Way BH23 14 C5
Ash Gro, Lymington SO41 24 A5
Ash Gro, Ringwood BH24 25 D3
Ash Gro, Southampton SO40 4 B3
Ash Rd SO40 4 A4
Ashburn Garth BH24 25 F3
Ashburton Cl SO45 16 C3
Ashby Cres SO40 26 C4
Ashby Rd SO40 26 C4
Ashdene Rd SO40 4 B3
Ashdown SO45 10 B2
Ashdown Rd SO45 10 B2
Ashdown Walk BH25 23 D5
Ashford Cl SP6 11 C3
Ashford Cres SO45 17 G3
Ashford Rd SP6 11 C3
Ashford Works Ind Est SP6 11 C3
Ashington Pk BH25 23 D5
Ashleigh Cl SO45 17 F6
Ashlet Gdns BH25 22 E3
Ashlett Cl SO45 10 D2
Ashlett Mws SO45 10 D2
Ashlett Rd SO45 10 D2
Ashley Arnewood Ct*, Ashley Rd BH25 22 D4
Ashley Cl BH24 25 E4
Ashley Common Rd BH25 22 D2
Ashley La, Hordle SO41 24 A1
Ashley La, Lymington SO41 19 F3
Ashley La, New Milton BH25 22 E3
Ashley Meads BH25 22 E3
Ashley Rd BH25 22 C4
Ashmore Av BH25 23 C6
Ashmore Gro BH23 14 C3
Ashtree Cl BH25 22 E4
Ashurst Bridge Rd SO40 26 B6
Ashurst Cl SO40 4 B3
Ashwood Gdns SO40 26 C5
Aspen Pl BH25 23 C6
Aspen Walk SO40 26 C5
Asquith Cl BH23 12 D5
Astra Ct SO45 17 F1
Atheling Rd SO45 17 F3
Aubrey Cl SO41 22 F3
Auckland Av SO42 7 C4
Auckland Pl SO42 7 C4
Auckland Rd BH23 14 A5
Audemer Ct BH24 25 E2
Austen Cl SO40 26 C5
Auster Cl BH23 13 G3
Autumn Copse BH25 22 E4
Avenue Rd, Brockenhurst SO42 7 C4
Avenue Rd, Christchurch BH23 15 F3

Avenue Rd, Lymington SO41 19 E3
Avenue Rd, New Milton BH25 22 B4
Avon Bldgs BH23 12 B3
Avon Cl SO41 18 D3
Avon Ct SP6 11 E3
Avon Meade SP6 11 D2
Avon Rd East BH23 12 A2
Avon Run Cl BH23 13 G5
Avon Run Rd BH23 13 H5
Avon Trading Pk BH23 12 A3
Avon Wharf BH23 12 C4
Aysha Cl BH25 23 C5

B Avenue SO45 10 A1
Back La, Brockenhurst SO42 7 D4
Back La, Lymington SO41 6 C5
Back La, Ringwood BH24 25 F3
Baden Cl BH25 23 D5
Badgers Cl SO41 6 C5
Badgers Copse BH25 22 D1
Badgers Walk SO45 17 E5
Badminton Drove SO45 10 D4
Bagber Rd SO40 27 E4
Bailey Cl BH25 22 E3
Baldwin Cl SO41 12 D4
Balfour Cl BH23 14 A4
Ballard Cl, New Milton BH25 22 C3
Ballard Cl, Southampton SO16 27 H3
Balmer Lawn Rd SO42 7 D1
Balmoral Ct BH23 15 E5
Balmoral Walk BH25 22 A4
Bank Cl BH25 22 B4
Bankhill Dr SO41 19 E1
Bankview SO41 19 E1
Barclay Mws SO45 17 F6
Bargates BH23 12 A3
Baring Rd BH6 12 A6
Barleycorn Walk SO40 9 B2
Barnes La SO41 21 D1
Barney Hayes La SO40 27 H3
Barnfield BH23 14 A5
Barnsfield Cres SO40 26 C4
Barrs Av BH25 22 C3
Barrs Wood Dr BH25 22 C3
Barrs Wood Rd BH25 22 D3
Bartley Av SO40 26 D5
Barton Cft BH25 23 B7
Barton Common La BH25 23 C7
Barton Common Rd BH25 23 C8
Barton Court Av BH25 23 B8
Barton Court Rd BH25 23 B6
Barton Dr BH25 23 A7
Barton Grn BH25 23 A7
Barton Ho BH25 15 H6
Barton La BH25 15 H4
Barton Way BH25 23 A7
Barton Wood Rd BH25 23 A8
Bartons Rd SP6 11 E3
Bartonside Rd BH25 15 F5
Bartram Rd SO40 27 F5
Bashley Cross Rd BH25 22 A2
Bashley Dr BH25 22 C1
Bashley Rd BH25 22 B1
Bath Rd SO41 19 G4
Batten Cl BH23 12 D3
Bay Tree Way BH23 18 D3
Bays Rd SO41 18 C3
Beach Av BH25 23 A8
Beacon Cl SO41 24 A5
Beacon Ct, Christchurch BH23 14 D5
Beacon Ct, Fordingbridge SP6 11 E2
Beacon Dr BH23 14 D5
Beaconsfield Rd BH23 12 B3
Bearslane Cl SO40 26 C2
Beatty Cl BH24 25 E2
Beauchamp Pl SO40 12 A3
Beaufort Cl BH23 13 H3

Beaulieu Cl BH25 15 H1
Beaulieu Rd, Lyndhurst SO43 20 C4
Beaulieu Rd, Southampton SO45 16 D6
Beaumaris Gdns SO45 17 E2
Beaver Ind Est BH23 13 F4
Beckley Copse BH23 15 E3
Becton La BH25 23 C8
Becton Mead BH25 23 C6
Bedford Cl BH23 11 E2
Beech Cl SO41 24 A5
Beech Rd SO40 4 B3
Beechcroft La BH24 25 C2
Beechdale Cl SO40 26 C1
Beechdale Walk SO40 26 C1
Beechen La SO43 20 C5
Beechwood Av BH25 22 A3
Beechwood La BH24 8 D2
Beechwood Rd SO40 9 B4
Beechwood Way SO45 16 C4
Belfield Rd BH6 12 A6
Bell Cl SO45 10 A3
Bellflower Cl BH23 13 G2
Belmont Cl SO45 17 F5
Belmont Rd BH25 22 B3
Belmore La SO41 19 E4
Belmore Rd SO41 19 E4
Belstone Rd SO40 27 E4
Belvedere Rd, Christchurch BH23 12 A3
Belvedere Rd, Southampton SO45 17 F5
Benbow Gdns SO40 26 C1
Benmore Cl BH25 23 E5
Bennetts La BH24 8 F3
Benson Cl BH23 6 C2
Beresford Gdns BH23 13 E4
Beresford Rd SO41 18 C3
Bermuda Cl BH25 15 E5
Bernwood Gro SO45 10 A6
Berryfield Rd SO41 24 C3
Bertram Rd BH25 22 D3
Betsy Cl BH23 6 C1
Betsy La BH23 6 C1
Beverley Rd SO45 17 E6
Bevis Cl SO45 10 B3
Bickerley Gdns BH24 25 B4
Bickerley Rd BH24 25 A3
Bickerley Ter BH24 25 A3
Bilberry Cl BH23 13 F4
Billington Pl SO41 18 D5
Bingham Cl BH23 13 E3
Bingham Dr SO41 19 F3
Bingham Rd BH23 12 D3
Birch Gro BH25 23 C6
Birchdale SO45 17 G5
Birchglade SO40 26 C2
Birchlands SO40 26 D6
Birchwood Cl BH23 14 C4
Birchy Hill SO41 6 C6
Bishop Ct BH23 13 F4
Bishops Cl SO40 26 D3
Bisterne Cl, Ringwood BH24 8 F3
Bisterne Cl, Ringwood BH24 8 F4
Bitterne Way SO41 19 E5
Blackberry La BH23 13 E4
Blackbird Way BH23 6 D2
Blackbush Rd SO41 21 C2
Blackdown Cl SO45 16 D4
Blackfield Rd SO45 10 A4
Blackthorn Cl SO41 18 B5
Blackthorn Way BH25 22 E3
Blackwater Dr SO40 26 C2
Blackwater Mws SO40 26 C3
Blair Cl BH25 22 A1
Blandford Cl SO41 21 D2
Blenheim Cl SO41 24 A1
Blenheim Cres SO41 24 A1
Blenheim Dr BH23 13 G4
Blenheim Gdns SO45 16 C5
Blenheim Mws SO45 17 F6
Bluebell Cl BH23 13 H2
Blythswood Ct BH25 23 B7
Boakes Pl SO40 4 B3

Bockhampton Rd BH23
Bodowen Rd BH23
Boldre Cl BH25
Bond Cl SO41
Boniface Cl SO40
Bonington Cl BH23
Boothby Cl SO40
Boundstone SO45
Bourne La SO40
Bourne Rd SO40
Bournemouth Rd SO43
Bouverie Cl SO41
Bowater Cl SO40
Bowater Way SO40
Bowerwood Rd SP6
Bowland Rise BH25
Bowling Green Rd SO41
Brabazon Dr BH23
Bracken Way BH23
Brackens Way SO41
Brackley Way SO40
Braehead SO45
Braemar Av BH6
Braemar Cl BH6
Braemar Dr BH23
Bramble Ct*, Fairview Par SO45
Bramble La BH23
Bramble Walk SO41
Bramble Way BH23
Bramley Cl SO41
Bramshaw Way BH25
Bramshott Hill SO45
Branders Cl BH6
Branders La BH6
Branksome Cl BH25
Bransgore Gdns BH23
Branwell Cl BH23
Branwood Cl SO41
Braxton Courtyard SO41
Breamore Cl BH25
Brecon Cl, New Milton BH25
Brecon Cl, Southampton SO45
Brendon Cl SO45
Briar Cl BH23
Briar Cl SO45
Briardene Ct SO40
Briarswood Rise SO45
Briarwood Rd SO40
Brickfield La SO41
Bridge St, Christchurch BH23
Bridge St, Fordingbridge SP6
Brighton Rd SO41
Brinton La SO45
Britannia Way BH23
Broad La SO41
Broadfields Cl SO41
Broadlands Cl SO41
Broadlands Rd SO42
Broadly Cl SO41
Broadmead Cl SO41
Broadmeadow Cl SO40
Broadshard Ct BH24
Broadshard La BH24
Broadway BH6
Brockhills La BH25
Brockishill Rd SO40
Brocks Cl SO45
Brokenford Av SO40
Brokenford La SO40
Bronte Av BH23
Bronte Cl SO40
Brook Av BH25
Brook Av North BH25
Brook La BH23
Brook Rd SO41
Brook Ter SP6
Brook Walk BH23
Brook Way BH23
Brookland Cl SO41
Brookley Rd SO42
Brooklyn Ct BH25

...oks Cl BH24 — 25 D4
...okside SO40 — 27 E6
...okside Cl BH23 — 6 B2
...okside Rd,
...ockenhurst SO42 — 7 C3
...okside Rd,
...ristchurch BH23 — 6 B1
...omfield La SO41 — 19 E2
...omhill Cl SO41 — 18 B5
...omy Cl SO45 — 16 C3
...ughton Rd SO43 — 20 B2
...wnhill Way SO16 — 27 H1
...wning Cl SO40 — 26 C5
...wnings Cl SO41 — 18 B3
...wnsea Cl BH25 — 22 A4
...nel Rd,
...dbridge SO15 — 27 H4
...nel Rd,
...uthampton SO40 — 26 C1
...nel Rd,
...tton SO40 — 27 E1
...nswick Pl SO41 — 19 E3
...shwood Ct BH23 — 14 B5
...yn Ct SP6 — 11 F3
...yn Rd SP6 — 11 F3
...mpton Cl SP6 — 11 C3
...e La BH23 — 13 E4
...rcaneers Cl BH23 — 12 D4
...ehayes Cl BH23 — 14 D5
...han Ct SO45 — 16 C4
...kingham Ct BH23 — 15 E5
...kingham Walk
...25 — 22 A4
...kland Dene SO41 — 19 E1
...kland Gdns SO40 — 26 B1
...kland Gro BH23 — 14 B3
...kstone Cl SO41 — 24 B4
...kthorn Cl SO40 — 26 A3
...downe Walk SO41 — 6 B4
...finch Cl SO40 — 26 B4
...rush Cl SO45 — 17 E5
...dock Cl BH23 — 13 H1
...e Cl BH23 — 13 H4
...e Haven Dr BH23 — 13 G5
...e Homage Gdns
...23 — 13 G4
...e Homage La
...23 — 13 G4
...e La BH23 — 13 G5
...e Pk BH23 — 13 H4
...ford La SO42 — 7 D2
...gate Flds SP6 — 11 F2
...ley Cl,
...ew Milton BH25 — 15 G4
...ley Cl,
...uthampton SO40 — 26 A4
...ley Lawn BH24 — 8 D2
...ley Rd,
...ockenhurst SO42 — 7 A4
...ley Rd,
...ristchurch BH23 — 6 A3
...nett Cl SO45 — 17 G4
...nham Rd SP6 — 11 E2
...nleigh Gdns BH25 — 22 E3
...nside BH23 — 14 B5
...ent House La BH23 — 6 B1
...rard Gro SO41 — 19 F5
...ton Cl BH23 — 12 C1
...ton Rd BH23 — 12 D3
...shells Fm SP6 — 11 E4
...e Dr BH23 — 15 F5
...lers La BH24 — 25 E1
...tercup Cl SO45 — 17 F5
...tercup Dr BH23 — 13 H1
...ts Ash Av SO45 — 17 F6
...ts Ash Gdns SO45 — 17 F6
...ts Ash La SO45 — 17 F6
...ts Bridge Hill SO45 — 17 F4
...ts Bridge Rd SO45 — 17 F5
...ts Lawn SO42 — 7 C2
...The Wood SO40 — 26 C1
...eways SO45 — 17 E4
...Pass Rd SO40 — 27 F5
...on Rd BH25 — 15 H4

...avenue SO45 — 10 A1
...oot Dr SO45 — 16 C3
...oot Way BH25 — 22 A4
...hay Cl BH25 — 22 A4
...inam La SO40 — 9 A1
...logan Rd SO40 — 25 C3
...af Av BH25 — 22 D4
...edonia Dr SO45 — 16 C3
...edonian Cl BH23 — 13 H3
...on Cl BH23 — 12 A1
...more Cres SO40 — 26 A2

Calmore Dr SO40 — 26 B2
Calmore Gdns SO40 — 26 C4
Calmore Rd SO40 — 26 B1
Calpe Av SO43 — 20 B3
Calshot Rd SO45 — 10 D2
Cambria Dr SO45 — 16 C3
Camden Hurst SO41 — 21 B3
Camellia Gdns BH25 — 22 C3
Cameron Rd BH23 — 12 D3
Camilla Cl SO40 — 26 A2
Campion Gro BH23 — 13 E4
Campion Way SO41 — 19 E1
Cannon St SO41 — 19 F3
Canons Walk SO41 — 21 E2
Canterbury Dr SO45 — 16 C3
Canute Dr BH23 — 6 C1
Capella Gdns SO45 — 16 D3
Capesthorne BH23 — 13 G5
Captains Row SO41 — 19 F5
Careys Cotts SO42 — 7 C2
Carisbrooke Ct,
  Christchurch BH23 — 15 E5
Carisbrooke Ct,
  New Milton BH25 — 22 A4
Carisbrooke Way
  BH23 — 14 C4
Carlton Av BH25 — 15 H5
Caroline Av BH23 — 13 E5
Carpenter Cl,
  Lymington SO41 — 19 E2
Carpenter Cl,
  Southampton SO45 — 17 F3
Carradale BH23 — 13 H2
Carrick Way BH25 — 23 D5
Carrington Cl SO41 — 21 F3
Carrington La SO41 — 21 F3
Carvers La BH24 — 25 B3
Carvers Trading Est
  BH24 — 25 B3
Caslake Cl BH25 — 23 B6
Castle Av BH23 — 14 C5
Castle Cl SO41 — 21 E4
Castle Ct BH23 — 15 E5
Castle Hill La BH24 — 8 A2
Castle St BH23 — 12 B4
Castleman Way BH24 — 25 B4
Catalina Cl BH23 — 13 G4
Cathay Gdns SO45 — 16 C3
Causeway Cres SO40 — 27 F4
Cavalier Cl SO45 — 16 C3
Cavendish Cnr Caravan Pk
  BH24 — 25 D2
Caxton Cl BH23 — 13 F3
Cecil Av BH23 — 4 B3
Cedar Dr SO41 — 24 A5
Cedar Gdns BH25 — 23 A6
Cedar Mt SO43 — 20 B4
Cedar Pl BH23 — 6 C1
Cedarwood Cl SO40 — 26 D3
Cedric Cl SO45 — 10 B5
Celandine Cl BH23 — 13 H2
Centenary Cl SO41 — 6 C5
Centenary Ho BH23 — 12 A3
Centre La BH24 — 24 B4
Centre Pl BH24 — 25 E2
Chaffey Cl BH24 — 25 E2
Chaffinch Cl,
  New Milton BH25 — 22 A4
Chaffinch Cl,
  Southampton SO40 — 26 B3
Chalewood Rd SO45 — 10 A6
Challenger Way SO45 — 16 C4
Chaloner Cres SO45 — 17 F6
Champion Cl SO41 — 21 F3
Channel Ct BH25 — 15 H5
Chant Cl BH23 — 13 G5
Chantry Cl BH23 — 14 C3
Chapel La,
  Blackfield SO45 — 10 A6
Chapel La,
  Christchurch BH23 — 6 B2
Chapel La,
  Fawley SO45 — 10 B2
Chapel La,
  Lymington SO41 — 19 E5
Chapel La,
  Lyndhurst SO43 — 20 B4
Chapel La,
  Ringwood BH24 — 8 C3
Chapel La,
  Southampton SO40 — 4 D1
Charing Cl BH24 — 25 C4
Chariot Cl SO45 — 16 C3
Charles Cres BH25 — 22 D2
Charles Ley Ct SO45 — 10 C2
Charles Rd BH23 — 13 F2
Charleston Rd SO41 — 17 H6
Charlotte Cl BH23 — 13 H5
Charlton Cl SO41 — 24 A2

Charmus Rd SO40 — 26 B2
Charnock Cl SO41 — 24 A2
Charnwood Cl SO40 — 26 C3
Charnwood Dr SP6 — 11 E2
Chatsworth Way BH25 — 15 H1
Chaucer Dr SO41 — 21 D3
Chaucombe Pl BH25 — 23 A6
Chaveney Cl SO45 — 17 E6
Cheam Way SO40 — 26 D2
Chepstow Cl SO40 — 26 A2
Chequers Cl SO41 — 18 C4
Cherry Tree Cl SO41 — 24 B5
Cherry Tree Ct*,
  Station Rd BH25 — 23 C5
Cherrywood Gdns
  SO40 — 26 B4
Chestnut Av BH25 — 23 B7
Chestnut Dr SO40 — 4 C3
Chestnut Rd SO42 — 7 D3
Cheviot Cl BH23 — 13 E2
Cheviot Dr SO45 — 16 C3
Chewton Common Rd
  BH23 — 14 D3
Chewton Farm Rd
  BH23 — 15 F4
Chewton Lodge BH23 — 15 F4
Chewton Way BH23 — 15 E3
Chichester Rd BH24 — 25 E2
Chichester Way BH23 — 13 G6
Chillenden Ct SO40 — 26 C6
Chiltern Cl,
  New Milton BH25 — 23 A6
Chiltern Cl,
  Southampton SO40 — 4 D1
Chiltern Ct*,
  Hunt Rd BH23 — 13 F2
Chiltern Dr BH25 — 15 H4
Chinham Rd SO40 — 9 D3
Christchurch Bay Rd
  BH25 — 23 A8
Christchurch By-Pass
  BH23 — 12 B3
Christchurch Rd,
  Christchurch BH23 — 15 F4
Christchurch Rd,
  Lymington SO41 — 24 A5
Christchurch Rd,
  New Milton BH25 — 23 A6
Christchurch Rd,
  Ringwood BH24 — 8 D3
Church Fm SP6 — 11 E4
Church Hill SP6 — 21 E3
Church La,
  Brockenhurst SO42 — 7 D4
Church La,
  Christchurch BH23 — 12 B4
Church La,
  Lymington SO41 — 19 E3
Church La,
  Lyndhurst SO43 — 20 C4
Church La,
  New Milton BH25 — 23 A5
Church La,
  Ringwood BH24 — 8 D3
Church La,
  Southampton SO45 — 10 B2
Church La, Sway SO41 — 6 C6
Church Mead SO41 — 19 F5
Church St,
  Christchurch BH23 — 12 B4
Church St,
  Fordingbridge SP6 — 11 E4
Churchfields SO45 — 10 D1
Churchill Ct BH23 — 23 A5
Claire Ct BH23 — 14 D5
Clare Gdns SO40 — 10 A6
Clare Lodge Cl BH23 — 6 B2
Clarence Pl BH23 — 12 A3
Clarence Rd SO43 — 20 C3
Clarendon Pk SO41 — 18 D5
Clarendon Rd BH23 — 14 D3
Clarks Cl BH24 — 25 B3
Clausen Way SO41 — 18 D6
Clay Hill SO45 — 20 C5
Claypits La SO45 — 16 B4
Clematis Cl BH23 — 13 H2
Cleveland Cl BH23 — 15 H5
Cleveland Dr SO45 — 16 D5
Cliff Cres BH25 — 23 A8
Cliff Dr BH23 — 15 G4
Cliff Rd SO41 — 21 A2
Cliff Ter BH25 — 23 A8
Cliffe Rd BH25 — 15 H5
Clinton Cl BH23 — 15 E3
Clinton Rd SO41 — 19 E2
Clive Rd BH23 — 14 B3
Clough La BH24 — 8 C3
Cloughs Rd BH24 — 25 C3
Clover Cl BH23 — 13 H2

Clover Ct BH25 — 22 E3
Clover Nooke SO15 — 27 H3
Clydesdale Way SO40 — 26 B4
Coastguard Cotts
  BH25 — 15 H5
Coastguard Way BH23 — 13 E6
Coat Gdns SO45 — 17 F3
Coblands Av SO40 — 26 C4
Cocklydown La SO40 — 4 D1
Colborne Cl SO41 — 19 E1
Colbourne Cl BH23 — 6 B2
Colemere Gdns BH23 — 14 C4
Coleridge Grn BH23 — 13 F3
Coleville Av SO45 — 10 C2
College Rd BH24 — 25 B3
Collins La BH24 — 25 B3
Collyers Rd SO42 — 7 C5
Columbine Cl BH23 — 13 H1
Comet Way BH23 — 13 G4
Commercial Rd SO40 — 27 F4
Compton Rd,
  New Milton BH25 — 23 B5
Compton Rd,
  Southampton SO40 — 27 F4
Conference Pl SO41 — 19 F5
Conifer Cl SO45 — 17 E3
Conifer Cres SO41 — 18 C4
Coniston Rd,
  Ringwood BH24 — 25 C4
Coniston Rd,
  Southampton SO16 — 27 H3
Connaught Cl BH25 — 15 H4
Conway Cl BH25 — 22 D4
Cook Cl BH24 — 25 E2
Cooks La SO40 — 26 B1
Coombe La SO41 — 6 D5
Cooper Rd SO40 — 4 B3
Copinger Cl SO40 — 26 C5
Copperfields SO40 — 26 B5
Coppice Cl BH25 — 22 E3
Coppice Rd SO40 — 26 C1
Copse Av BH23 — 23 C5
Copse Cl, Hythe SO45 — 17 E5
Copse Cl,
  Southampton SO40 — 27 E6
Copse Rd,
  New Milton BH25 — 22 C4
Copse Rd,
  Ringwood BH24 — 8 C4
Copse Way BH23 — 14 B4
Copsewood Rd,
  Ashurst SO40 — 4 B2
Copsewood Rd,
  Hythe SO45 — 17 E3
Copthorne La SO45 — 10 D2
Corbin Rd SO41 — 18 B4
Corbould Rd SO45 — 17 E6
Cordelia Cl SO45 — 16 D3
Coriander Dr SO40 — 26 D3
Corinna Gdns SO45 — 16 D3
Cormorant Dr SO45 — 17 H4
Cornflower Dr BH23 — 13 H1
Cornford Way BH23 — 14 B5
Cornforth Rd SO40 — 26 B2
Cornwallis Rd SO41 — 21 C3
Corsair Dr SO45 — 16 D3
Cosworth Dr SO45 — 16 D4
Cotswold Cl SO45 — 16 D4
Cotswold Ct*,
  Hunt Rd BH23 — 13 F2
Cott La BH24 — 25 B3
Cottage Mws SP6 — 11 E3
Cottagers La SO41 — 24 B2
Court Cl,
  Christchurch BH23 — 12 D4
Court Cl,
  Lymington SO41 — 19 E5
Court Cl,
  Southampton SO40 — 26 C1
Courtenay Pl SO41 — 19 E4
Courtier Cl SO45 — 16 D3
Cowley Rd SO41 — 18 C3
Cowper Av BH25 — 23 B6
Coxstone La BH24 — 25 B3
Crabapple Cl SO40 — 26 D5
Crabbs Way SO40 — 26 A4
Cranborne Pl BH25 — 22 A4
Cranemoor Av BH23 — 14 C3
Cranemoor Cl BH23 — 14 C2
Cranemoor Gdns
  BH23 — 14 C3
Cranwell Cl BH23 — 6 C2
Creedy Dr BH23 — 12 A5
Creedy Path BH23 — 12 B4
Crescent Cl BH23 — 23 A8
Crescent Dr BH23 — 23 A8
Crete Cotts SO45 — 17 E6
Crete La SO45 — 17 E6
Crete Rd SO45 — 17 E6

Cricket Cl BH23 — 13 F5
Cringle Av BH6 — 12 A6
Crispin Cl BH23 — 14 D4
Crittall Cl SO41 — 6 C5
Crockford Cl BH25 — 22 C2
Croft Rd,
  Christchurch BH23 — 13 F3
Croft Rd,
  Ringwood BH24 — 25 E1
Cromalt Cl SO45 — 16 C4
Crooked La BH25 — 23 D7
Crossmead Av BH25 — 23 B5
Crossways SO41 — 24 A5
Crow Arch La BH24 — 25 C4
Crow Arch La Ind Est
  BH24 — 25 C4
Crow La BH24 — 25 D4
Cruse Cl SO41 — 6 B5
Cuckmere La SO16 — 27 H3
Cuckoo Hill Way BH23 — 6 D2
Culford Av SO40 — 27 E5
Culford Way SO40 — 27 E5
Cull La BH25 — 22 C1
Cullwood La BH25 — 22 D2
Culver Rd BH25 — 23 A5
Culverley Cl SO42 — 7 C4
Cumberland Way
  SO45 — 16 C3
Cunningham Cl,
  Christchurch BH23 — 13 F4
Cunningham Cl,
  Ringwood BH24 — 25 E2
Cunningham Ct*,
  Nelson Cl BH25 — 22 A4
Curlew Cl SO45 — 17 H5
Curlew Dr SO45 — 17 G4
Curlew Rd BH23 — 13 F4
Curlew Walk SO45 — 17 G4
Curzon Cl SO41 — 18 D5
Curzon Way BH23 — 14 B5
Cutler Cl BH25 — 22 E3
Cygnus Gdns SO45 — 16 B3
Cypress Gdns SO40 — 26 B5
Cypress Gro SO41 — 24 B5
Cyprus Av SO40 — 4 C3

D Avenue SO45 — 10 C1
Dacres Walk SO41 — 21 E2
Dairy Cl BH23 — 12 D4
Dakota Cl BH23 — 13 G3
Dale Rd SO45 — 17 E3
Dales Way SO40 — 26 B4
Dane Cl SO45 — 10 B4
Dane Rd SO41 — 21 A1
Danecrest Rd SO41 — 24 A2
Danes Cl BH23 — 23 B7
Danesbury Mdws
  BH25 — 22 D2
Danestream Cl SO41 — 21 D3
Danestream Ct SO41 — 21 E3
Daneswood Rd BH25 — 22 D4
Daniells Cl SO41 — 19 F4
Daniells Walk SO41 — 19 E4
Daniels Walk SO40 — 26 B3
Dark La,
  Christchurch BH23 — 14 D1
Dark La,
  New Milton BH25 — 22 A3
Dark La,
  Southampton SO45 — 10 A4
Davidson Cl SO45 — 17 G2
Davis Fld BH25 — 22 A4
Dawkins Way BH25 — 23 B5
Dayrell Cl SO40 — 26 B2
De Havilland Way
  BH23 — 13 F5
De La Warr Rd SO41 — 21 C3
De Mowbray Way
  SO41 — 19 E5
Deans Ct SO41 — 21 D3
Dearing Cl SO43 — 20 C4
Deer Park Cl BH25 — 22 A3
Deerhurst Cl SO40 — 26 C5
Deerleap Cl SO45 — 17 F4
Deerleap La SO40 — 4 C3
Deerleap Way,
  New Milton BH25 — 22 C1
Deerleap Way,
  Southampton SO45 — 17 F4
Delft Mws*,
  Scotts Hills La BH23 — 12 A1
Delta Cl BH23 — 13 G3
Denbigh Cl SO40 — 26 C6
Dene Cl BH24 — 25 E1
Dene Rd SO40 — 4 B3
Dene Way SO40 — 4 B3
Deneside Copse SO41 — 18 C1
Denham Dr BH23 — 14 C4
Denholm Cl BH24 — 25 E1

Denmead BH25 22 E3
Dennistoun Av BH23 13 E3
Denny Cl SO45 10 C2
Deridene Ct SO40 26 C5
Derritt La BH23 6 A2
Derrybrian Gdns BH25 23 C5
Derwent Dr SO40 26 B3
Derwent Rd BH25 22 C2
Deverel Cl BH23 12 A2
Devonshire Gdns SO45 17 F6
Deweys La BH24 25 A3
Diamond Cl SP6 11 E4
Diamond Cl SP6 11 E4
Diana Ct BH23 14 D5
Dibden Lodge Cl SO45 17 F6
Dickens Dell SO40 26 A5
Dilly La BH24 23 B7
Dinham Ct BH25 22 E3
Dinham Rd BH25 22 E3
Disraeli Rd BH23 12 D4
Ditchbury SO41 19 E1
Dock La SO42 5 D3
Doe Copse Way BH25 22 A3
Dolphin Pl BH25 23 B8
Dominy Cl SO45 17 G2
Donnington Dr BH23 13 H3
Dorland Gdns SO40 26 C5
Dorset Rd BH23 13 E2
Douglas Way SO41 17 E2
Doveys Cl BH24 8 C3
Downs Park Av SO40 27 F6
Downs Park Cres SO40 27 F6
Downs Park Rd SO40 27 F6
Downton La SO41 21 A2
Downwood Cl, Fordingbridge SP6 11 C3
Downwood Cl, Southampton SO45 16 C5
Drake Cl, Christchurch BH23 13 F4
Drake Cl, New Milton BH25 22 A4
Drake Cl, Ringwood BH24 25 E1
Drakes Cl SO45 17 E4
Draper Rd BH23 13 E3
Drayton Pl SO40 26 D5
Driftwood Gdns SO40 26 B5
Druitt Rd BH23 13 E2
Drummond Rd SO45 17 F2
Dryden Pl SO41 21 D2
Duart Ct BH25 25 D4
Duck Island La BH24 25 B4
Ducking Stool La BH23 12 B4
Dudley Av, Fordingbridge SP6 11 E2
Dudley Av, Lymington SO41 24 A3
Dudley Pl*, Station Rd BH25 23 C5
Dukeswood Dr SO45 17 F5
Dunbar Cres BH23 14 D3
Duncan Rd BH25 22 E3
Duncliff Rd BH6 12 A6
Dunedin Gro BH24 14 A5
Dunfield Copse SO45 10 B3
Dunford Cl BH25 15 H4
Dunlin Cl BH23 13 G5
Durland Cl BH25 23 B5
Durley Cres SO40 26 D6
Durlston Rd SO16 27 H2
Durnstown SO41 6 C5
Durrant Way SO41 9 B1

Earley Ct SO41 19 F3
Earlsdon Way BH23 14 C4
Earlswood Park BH25 22 E2
East Av BH25 15 G5
East Bank Rd SO42 7 A3
East Cl BH25 15 H4
East Cliff Way BH23 14 A5
East Hill SO41 19 E3
East La SO41 24 B5
East View Rd BH24 25 C3
Eastern Rd SO41 19 E3
Eastern Way SO41 21 F3
Eastfield Ct BH24 25 D3
Eastfield La BH24 25 D3
Eastlands BH25 23 D5
Eastmeare Ct SO40 26 B5
Ebenezer La BH24 25 B5
Eddystone Rd SO40 26 C1
Edmunds Cl BH25 23 B6
Edward Cl SO45 10 A4

Edward Rd, Christchurch BH23 13 F2
Edward Rd, Southampton SO45 17 F2
Edwards Cl SO41 18 C4
Edwina Cl BH24 25 D1
Efford Ct SO41 18 C5
Efford Way SO41 18 B5
Elcombes Cl SO43 20 B4
Elderberry La BH23 13 F4
Eldon Av BH25 23 A6
Eldon Cl BH25 15 H4
Elgar Cl SO41 19 F3
Elgin Cl SO45 17 G4
Eling Hill SO40 27 G6
Eling La SO40 27 F5
Elizabeth Cres SO41 24 C3
Elizabeth Gdns, Christchurch BH23 14 A5
Elizabeth Gdns, Southampton SO45 17 F5
Elkhams Cl SO41 24 A5
Elldene Ct SO40 26 D6
Ellery Gro SO41 19 E2
Ellingham Rd BH25 15 G5
Elliot Cl SO40 26 C5
Elm Av, Lymington SO41 18 D5
Elm Av, New Milton BH25 23 B5
Elm Vw BH24 25 E4
Elmers Way BH23 6 C1
Elms Cl SP6 11 A2
Elmtree Cl SO40 4 B3
Elmwood Av SP6 11 C3
Elmwood Way BH23 14 D5
Elphinstone Rd BH23 13 E5
Elvin Cl SO41 24 A1
Embankment Way BH24 25 C4
Embley Cl SO40 26 C1
Emerald Cres SO45 17 G2
Empress Rd SO43 20 C3
Emsworth Rd SO41 19 F3
Endeavour Way SO41 17 F1
Enderwood Cl SO40 26 B3
Esdaile La BH24 8 C3
Ethelred Gdns SO40 26 C5
Euston Gro BH24 25 C4
Evergreens SO40 27 F5
Everlea Cl SO41 24 A4
Everon Gdns BH25 23 C5
Everton Rd, Everton SO41 24 A4
Everton Rd, Hordle SO41 24 A1
Ewart Ct SO45 17 F2
Ewell Way SO40 26 C2
Exeter Cl BH25 15 E5
Exmoor Cl SO40 26 A3
Eyeworth Walk SO45 16 B3
Eynon Mws BH24 25 B4
Eyre Cl SO41 26 D5

Fairfield BH23 12 A3
Fairfield Cl, Christchurch BH23 12 B3
Fairfield Cl, Lymington SO41 19 E4
Fairfield Cl, Southampton SO45 17 F3
Fairlea Rd SO41 19 F2
Fairlie BH24 25 D1
Fairlie Pk BH24 25 D1
Fairmead Way SO40 4 D1
Fairmile Rd BH23 12 A2
Fairview Cl SO45 17 F4
Fairview Dr SO45 17 F3
Fairview Par SO45 17 F4
Fairway Rd SO45 17 E3
Falcon Dr SO41 13 G5
Falcon Flds SO45 10 C2
Falstaff Way SO40 26 D6
Farm Cl BH24 25 B2
Farm La BH23 13 G5
Farm La North BH25 23 B7
Farm La South BH25 23 B7
Farmdene Cl BH23 14 B4
Farmers Walk SO41 24 A5
Farnleys Mead SO41 19 E5
Fathersfield SO42 7 C3
Fawcett Rd BH25 23 A5
Fawley By-Pass SO45 10 C2
Fawley Rd, Fawley SO45 10 A2
Fawley Rd, Hythe SO45 17 F6

Fawn Gdns BH25 22 A3
Felton Cres BH23 14 D4
Fennel Gdns SO41 19 E1
Fern Rd SO45 17 E4
Ferndale Rd BH25 22 C2
Fernglade BH25 22 C3
Fernhill La BH25 22 B1
Fernhill Rd BH25 22 B3
Fernhills Rd SO45 17 G5
Fernlea Way SO45 16 C4
Fernleigh Cl BH25 23 C6
Ferny Rd SO45 17 E3
Ferrypoint SO41 19 G3
Fibbards Rd SO42 7 C3
Field Pl BH25 15 G4
Field Walk SO41 18 D2
Field Way BH23 14 B4
Fieldfare Ct SO40 26 B3
Fieldway BH24 25 C2
Fifth St SO45 10 A2
Filton Cl SO40 26 B3
Filton Rd SO41 18 D2
Fir Av BH25 23 C5
Fir Cl SO43 20 B4
Fir Rd SO40 4 A3
Fir Tree La BH23 14 B3
Fir Tree Rd SO40 9 C2
Fire Station La SO42 5 C4
Firmount Cl SO41 24 B5
Firshill BH23 14 C4
First Marine Av BH25 23 B8
First St SO45 10 C2
Firtree Cres SO41 24 A2
Fishermans Bank BH23 13 E5
Fishermans Quay SO41 19 F3
Fishers Rd SO40 27 F5
Flambard Av BH23 12 A1
Flaxfields End SP6 11 D4
Fletcher Cl SO45 16 C3
Fletchwood La SO40 4 A3
Fletchwood Rd SO40 26 B5
Fleuret Cl SO45 17 F6
Floriston Gdns BH25 22 E4
Flowerdown Cl SO40 26 B3
Flushards SO41 19 G4
Foldsgate Cl SO43 20 B2
Fontwell Cl SO40 26 C2
Fordingbridge By-Pass SP6 11 F4
Forest Cl BH23 14 B3
Forest Ct, Fordingbridge SP6 11 F3
Forest Ct, New Milton BH25 22 C4
Forest Edge SO45 10 C2
Forest Edge Cl SO41 6 B4
Forest Front SO45 17 F6
Forest Gate SO45 10 B6
Forest Gate Gdns SO41 19 E6
Forest Gdns SO43 20 B3
Forest Glade Cl SO42 7 A3
Forest Hall SO42 7 D3
Forest Hill Way SO45 17 G5
Forest Hills Ct BH24 25 F4
Forest Oak Dr BH25 22 C2
Forest Park Rd SO42 7 B2
Forest Pines BH25 22 C2
Forest Rd BH24 8 A1
Forest Rise BH23 14 B3
Forest Vw SO42 7 A3
Forest Way, Christchurch BH23 14 A3
Forest Way, Lymington SO41 24 A4
Foresters Rd SO45 10 A3
Forestlake Av BH24 25 F4
Forestside Gdns BH24 25 E1
Forge La SO41 24 A4
Forge Rd SO45 10 A6
Forward Dr SO41 18 D5
Fountain Way BH23 12 B4
Fourshells Cl SO45 10 A3
Fourth St SO45 10 A2
Fox Fld SO41 24 B5
Fox Lease Ter SO43 20 B5
Fox Pond La SO41 24 A6
Foxbury Cl SO45 17 F5
Foxcote Gdns BH25 22 A4
Foxglove Cl BH23 13 H2
Foxglove Pl BH25 22 E3
Foxhayes La SO45 10 A6
Foxhills SO40 4 C2
Foxhills Cl SO40 4 B2
Foxlands SO45 10 A6
Foxs Walk SO45 10 A6
Foxtail Dr SO45 17 E5

Foxwood Av BH23 13 E5
Foxy Pad SO45 10 A6
Frampton Cl BH25 22 D2
Frampton Pl BH24 25 B3
Frampton Way SO40 27 E5
Frances Ct BH23 15 E5
Franklin Rd BH25 22 D3
Fraser Ct*, Marryat Rd BH25 22 A4
Frayslea SO45 17 F5
Freshwater Rd BH25 14 A6
Friars Cft SO40 26 B1
Friars Rd BH23 13 H4
Friars Walk BH25 23 B6
Fritham Cl SO40 26 C4
Frobisher Cl, Christchurch BH23 13 F4
Frobisher Cl, Ringwood BH24 25 E2
Froghall SO45 17 F5
Fromond Cl*, Campion Way SO41 19 E1
Frost La SO45 17 G4
Fry Cl SO45 10 B3
Frys La SO41 24 A4
Fullerton Rd SO41 18 D3
Fulmar Dr SO45 17 G4
Fulmar Rd BH23 13 G5
Furze Cft BH25 23 B5
Furzedale Gdns SO45 17 G5
Furzedale Pk SO45 17 G5
Furzedown Mws SO45 17 G5
Furzey Av SO45 17 G4
Furzey Cl SO45 10 A4
Furzy Whistlers Cl BH23 6 C1

Gainsborough Av BH25 22 C2
Gainsborough Ct SO41 18 D5
Galsworthy Rd SO40 26 C5
Gannet Cl SO45 17 G4
Garden City SO45 16 A1
Garden Cl, Lyndhurst SO43 20 A3
Garden Cl, New Milton BH25 23 B5
Garden Rd BH24 8 C3
Gardner Rd BH24 25 D4
Garendon Ct SP6 11 E2
Garrow Dr SO41 19 E2
Genoa Cl SO41 18 C6
George St SO45 10 A5
Georgian Cl BH24 25 D5
Georgina Cl SO40 26 A3
Germaine Cl BH23 13 H4
Gilbert Cl SO41 19 E5
Gillingham Rd SO41 21 E4
Gilpin Cl SO41 21 E4
Gilpin Hill SO41 6 B5
Gilpin Pl SO41 6 B4
Gipsy La BH24 25 D2
Gladstone Cl BH23 12 D4
Glebefields SO41 21 D3
Glen Cl BH25 15 G4
Glen Dr BH25 15 F5
Glen Rd SO40 27 F4
Glenavon BH25 23 D5
Glenavon Rd BH24 13 D3
Glendale Rd BH6 12 A6
Glendales BH25 15 G4
Glengarry BH25 23 D5
Glengarry Way BH23 13 H4
Glenside, New Milton BH25 15 F5
Glenside, Southampton SO45 17 E4
Glenville Cl BH23 15 E2
Glenville Rd BH23 15 E3
Glyn Jones Cl SO45 10 B3
Gold Mead Cl SO41 19 F4
Goldcrest La SO40 26 B4
Golden Cres SO41 24 A5
Golden Hind Pk SO45 17 E4
Goldfinch Cl BH23 23 A5
Goldsmith Cl SO40 26 C5
Goodwood Gdns SO40 26 C3
Goose Grn SO43 20 C5
Gooseberry La BH24 25 B3
Gordon Mt BH23 15 E4
Gordon Rd, Christchurch BH23 15 E4
Gordon Rd, Lymington SO41 18 C4
Gordon Way BH23 12 C1
Gore Grange BH25 23 A5

Gore Rd BH25 15
Gore Rd Ind Est BH25
Gorley Rd BH24 25
Gorse Cl BH25 22
Gorsefield Rd BH25 22
Gosport La SO43 20
Gosport St SO41 19
Gover Rd SO16 27
Graddidge Way SO40 26
Grafton Cl BH23 12
Grafton Gdns SO41 18
Grange Cl SO41 24
Grange Ct SO41 24
Grange Rd BH23 13
Grange Rd Bsns Centre BH23
Grasmere Gdns BH25 22
Gravel La BH24 25
Grays Av SO45 17
Great Mead SO43 20
Greatwood Cl SO45 17
Grebe Cl, Christchurch BH23 13
Grebe Cl, Lymington SO41 21
Green Acre BH25 23
Green Acres BH23 13
Green Cl SO45 17
Green La, Cadnam SO40 9
Green La, Fawley SO45 10
Green La, Fordingbridge SP6 11
Green La, Fordingbridge SP6 11
Green La, New Milton BH25 23
Green La, Ringwood BH24 25
Greenacres SO45 17
Greenbanks Cl SO41 21
Greenfield Gdns BH25
Greenfields Av SO40 27
Greenfields Cl SO40 27
Greenfinch Walk BH24 25
Greenmead Av SO41 24
Greenside Ct BH25 23
Greenway Cl SO41 18
Greenways, Christchurch BH23 13
Greenways, Lymington SO41 21
Greenways Rd SO42 7
Greenwoods BH25 23
Gregory Gdns SO40 26
Grenville Cl BH24 25
Grenville Gdns SO45 17
Griffin Ind Pk SO40 26
Grigg La SO42 7
Grosvenor Mws SO41 18
Grove Pastures SO41 19
Grove Pl SO41 19
Grove Rd, Lymington SO41 19
Grove Rd, New Milton BH25 23
Groveley Rd BH23 13
Guillemot Cl SO45 17
Guys Cl BH24

Haarlem Mws BH23 12
Haglane Copse SO41 18
Haking Rd BH23 12
Hale Av BH25 23
Hale Gdns BH25 23
Halifax Way BH23 13
Halton BH23 6
Haltons Cl SO40 26
Hambert Way SO40 26
Hamilton Cl BH23 13
Hamilton Ct SO41 21
Hamilton Mws SO45 17
Hammonds Cl SO40 26
Hammonds Grn SO40 26
Hammonds La SO40 26
Hammonds Way SO40
Hampton Cl BH25 10
Hampton Dr BH24 25
Hampton La SO45 10
Hamtun Cres SO40 27
Hamtun Gdns SO40
Handley Ct BH24 25
Harbour Cres BH25 23
Harbour Ct BH25

Entry	Ref
Harbour View Ct*, Princess Av BH23	12 B5
Hardy Cl, Christchurch BH23	13 F5
Hardy Cl, New Milton BH25	22 A4
Hardy Dr SO45	17 G5
Hare La, Lymington SO41	22 F3
Hare La, New Milton BH25	22 F4
Harford Cl SO41	18 C6
Harold Cl SO40	26 C5
Harriers Cl BH23	14 B4
Harrington Ct BH23	14 D5
Harris Way BH25	22 D1
Harry Barrows Cl BH24	25 B3
Hart Cl BH25	22 A3
Hart Hill SO45	17 H5
Hartley Cl SO45	17 F6
Hartley Walk SO45	17 F6
Harts Way SO45	24 A4
Hartsgrove Av SO45	10 A5
Hartsgrove Cl SO45	10 A5
Harvester Way SO41	19 E1
Harvey Gdns SO45	17 G3
Harwood Cl SO40	26 D4
Harwood Ct BH25	22 A4
Haselbury Rd SO40	27 E4
Haskells Cl SO43	20 B4
Haslemere Av BH23	14 D4
Haslemere Pl BH23	14 D4
Hatchet La SO42	5 A5
Hatfield Ct BH25	22 A3
Havelock Way BH23	14 B2
Haven Ct SO41	21 C3
Haven Gdns BH25	23 C5
Hawkers Cl SO40	27 E2
Hawkhill SO45	16 B3
Hawkins Cl, Christchurch BH23	13 F5
Hawkins Cl, Ringwood BH24	12 A1
Haworth Cl BH25	12 A1
Hawthorn Cl BH25	22 D3
Hawthorn Dr SO41	6 B5
Hawthorn Rd, Christchurch BH23	13 E2
Hawthorn Rd, Southampton SO45	17 E3
Hawthorne Rd SO43	26 C3
Haydens Ct SO41	19 F3
Haydock Cl SO40	26 C3
Hayley Cl SO45	17 F6
Haynes Way SO45	16 D5
Haysoms Cl BH25	23 C6
Hayward Cl SO40	26 C4
Hazel Cl BH23	14 A3
Hazel Ct*, Station Rd BH25	23 C5
Hazel Farm Rd SO40	26 B4
Hazel Rd SO41	18 B3
Hazelwood Av BH25	22 A3
Heart of Oak Mws SO41	19 E3
Heath Rd, Christchurch BH23	15 E3
Heath Rd, Lymington SO41	24 A2
Heather Cl, Christchurch BH23	15 E3
Heather Cl, Lymington SO41	24 B2
Heather Cl, Southampton SO40	26 D5
Heather Rd SO45	10 A3
Heatherstone Av SO45	17 E6
Heathfield SO45	17 E4
Heathwood Av BH25	15 H4
Heathy Cl BH25	23 A7
Hedgerley BH25	23 C7
Hedley Cl SO45	10 A4
Hemming SO40	27 E5
Hengistbury Rd BH25	15 H4
Herbert Rd BH25	22 C4
Heron Cl SO41	11 E2
Herons Wood SO40	26 C2
Hertford Cl SP6	11 E2
Hertford Ct BH23	15 E5
Hides Hill La SO42	5 B1
High Ridge Cres BH25	22 D4
High St, Brockenhurst SO42	5 B4
High St, Christchurch BH23	12 B4
High St, Fordingbridge SP6	11 E4
High St, Hythe SO45	17 F2
High St, Lymington SO41	19 E3
High St, Lyndhurst SO43	20 B4
High St, Milford on Sea SO41	21 E3
High St, Ringwood BH24	25 A3
High St, Southampton SO40	27 F5
Highbank Gdns SP6	11 E4
Highbury Cl BH25	22 C4
Highcliffe Rd BH23	13 G2
Highfield SO41	18 D4
Highfield Av, Lymington SO41	18 D4
Highfield Av, Ringwood BH24	25 B2
Highfield Cl SO41	6 B5
Highfield Dr BH24	25 C1
Highfield Gdns SO41	6 B5
Highfield Rd, Lymington SO41	18 C3
Highfield Rd, Ringwood BH24	25 B2
Highgrove Cl SO40	4 C1
Highland Av BH23	15 E4
Highlands Cl SO45	17 F5
Highlands Rd BH25	23 B7
Highlands Way SO45	17 F5
Hightown Gdns BH24	25 D4
Hightown Hill BH24	25 F4
Hightown Ind Est BH24	25 C4
Hightown Rd BH24	25 B4
Highwood Rd SO42	7 C4
Hill Cl BH23	6 B3
Hill La BH23	6 B3
Hillary Cl SO43	20 C6
Hillary Rd BH23	13 E2
Hillcroft Cl SO41	19 E3
Hillditch SO41	19 E1
Hillside Rd SO41	18 D4
Hillview Rd SO45	17 E3
Hiltom Rd BH24	25 C3
Hilton Rd BH25	22 D3
Hinton Wood Av BH23	14 C2
Hinton Wood La BH23	14 B2
Hirst Rd SO45	17 G4
Hives Way SO41	19 E1
Hobart Dr SO45	17 G3
Hobart Rd BH25	23 B5
Hoburne Gdns BH23	14 A4
Hoburne La BH23	13 H2
Holes Cl SO41	24 A1
Holland Rd SO40	26 B5
Hollands Wood Dr BH25	22 C2
Hollies Cl SO41	6 B6
Holly Gdns, Christchurch BH23	12 D1
Holly Gdns, Lymington SO41	21 C3
Holly Hatch Rd SO40	26 D5
Holly La, Christchurch BH23	15 F2
Holly La, New Milton BH25	22 E3
Holly Rd, Ashurst SO40	4 A4
Holly Rd, Fawley SO45	10 A5
Hollybank Cl SO45	17 F3
Hollybank Cres SO45	17 F2
Hollybank Rd SO45	17 E3
Hollywood La SO41	19 E2
Holm Cl BH24	25 E1
Holme Cl SO41	18 C5
Holme Rd BH23	15 E4
Holmhurst Av BH23	14 C3
Holmsley Cl SO41	18 B5
Holmsley Cl SO40	26 B3
Holmwood Garth BH24	25 D3
Home Farm Cl SO45	17 G4
Homefield SO43	20 C3
Homegrange Ho SO41	21 D4
Homewood Cl BH25	22 D4
Honey La BH24	8 B2
Honeybourne Cres BH6	12 A6
Honeysuckle Gdns SO41	24 A5
Honeysuckle Way BH23	13 G2
Honeywood Cl SO40	26 C2
Hordle La SO41	24 B3
Horlock Rd SO42	7 C3
Hotspur Cl SO45	17 E2
Hounsdown Av SO40	27 E6
Hounsdown Cl SO40	27 E6
House Mws*, Ellery Gro SO41	19 E2
Howard Cl, Christchurch BH23	13 F5
Howard Cl, Ringwood BH24	8 C3
Howards Mead SO41	18 C4
Howe Cl, Christchurch BH23	13 F5
Howe Cl, New Milton BH25	22 A4
Howlett Cl SO41	18 D2
Hudson Cl BH24	25 E2
Hudson Ct SO40	26 C5
Hughes Bsns Centre BH23	13 F3
Hungerfield Cl BH23	13 F3
Hunt Rd BH23	13 E2
Hunter Cl BH23	13 G3
Hunters Cres SO40	26 B5
Hunters Hill SO40	4 D2
Huntingdon Cl SO40	26 D2
Hurdles Mead SO41	21 E4
Hursley Dr SO45	10 A6
Hurst Cl, Christchurch BH23	15 F2
Hurst Cl, New Milton BH25	15 G4
Hurst Cl, Southampton SO40	27 F3
Hurst Ct, Christchurch BH23	15 E5
Hurst Ct, Lymington SO41	21 C3
Hurst Rd, Lymington SO41	21 E4
Hurst Rd, Ringwood BH24	25 B1
Hurstbourne Av BH23	14 C3
Huxley Cl SO45	16 C4
Hyde Cl, Lymington SO41	6 C5
Hyde Cl, Southampton SO40	26 B4
Hyman Way SO40	27 E4
Hynesbury Rd BH23	13 H4
Hythe By-Pass SO45	16 A1
Hythe Marina SO41	17 F1
Ibbotson Way SO40	4 D1
Imber Dr BH23	14 D4
Ingle Glen SO45	17 F5
Ingle Grn SO40	26 B3
Inglegreen Cl BH24	23 A6
Inglewood Dr BH25	23 D5
Inveravon BH23	13 F6
Ipley Way SO45	17 F5
Irvine Way BH23	13 E2
Island View Av BH23	13 G4
Island View Cl SO41	21 E4
Island View Ct BH23	23 B7
Island View Rd BH25	15 G5
Itchin Cl SO40	26 D5
Ivy Cl SO40	26 D2
Jackie Wigg Gdns SO40	27 F5
Jacmar Ct*, Ashley Rd BH25	22 C4
Jacobean Cl BH23	15 E3
Janes Cl SO40	10 A5
Janred Ct BH25	15 H5
Jasmine Ct SO41	19 E3
Jaundrells Cl BH25	22 D4
Jays Ct BH23	13 F4
Jellicoe Dr BH23	13 F4
Jennings Rd SO40	27 F4
Jesmond Av BH23	14 D5
Jessica Cres SO40	26 A2
Jessop Cl SO45	17 F1
Jessop Walk SO45	17 F1
Johnstone Rd BH23	13 E4
Jonathan Cl SO41	19 E2
Jones La SO45	17 F2
Jordans La SO41	6 C4
Jowitt Dr BH25	23 A5
Joyce Dickson Cl BH24	25 D4
Jubilee Cl, Fordingbridge SP6	11 C3
Jubilee Cl, Ringwood BH24	25 C3
Jubilee Ct SO41	6 B6
Jubilee Rd SP6	11 B3
Julia Cl BH23	14 C5
Junction Rd SO40	27 F5
Juniper Cl SO41	18 C5
Kathryn Cl SO40	26 A2
Kay Cl BH23	13 E4
Kayleigh Cl SO40	26 C5
Keats Av SO41	21 D3
Kelsall Gdns BH25	22 B4
Kelvin Cl SO45	17 F3
Kenilworth Cl BH25	22 C4
Kenilworth Ct*, Stour Rd BH23	12 A3
Kenmore Cl SO40	4 D1
Kennard Ct BH25	22 B4
Kennard Rd BH25	22 A3
Kenneth Ct BH23	15 E5
Kennington La SO40	9 D2
Kensington Flds SO45	16 D4
Kensington Pk SO41	21 D3
Kent Gdns SO40	26 D6
Keppel Cl BH24	25 D5
Kerry Cl SO41	18 C4
Kerry Gdns SP6	11 A3
Kestrel Cl BH24	25 B2
Kestrel Dr BH23	13 G4
Keswick Cl BH25	22 C2
Keswick Rd BH25	22 C2
Kewlake La SO40	9 A1
Keyes Cl BH23	13 F4
Keyhaven Rd SO41	21 F3
Keysworth Av BH25	23 A7
Kilmington Way BH23	14 C4
Kiln Cl SO45	17 E3
Kilnyard Cl SO40	26 C3
King George Mobile Home Pk BH24	23 A6
Kingfisher Way, Christchurch BH23	13 F5
Kingfisher Way, Ringwood BH24	25 D1
Kings Arms La BH24	25 A3
Kings Arms Row BH24	25 A3
Kings Av BH23	12 A4
Kings Cl, Lymington SO41	18 D3
Kings Cl, Lyndhurst SO43	20 B3
Kings Cres SO41	18 D2
Kings Ct SP6	11 E3
Kings Farm La SO41	24 C3
Kings Rd, Lymington SO41	18 D3
Kings Rd, New Milton BH25	22 D3
Kings Ride SO45	10 A6
Kings Saltern Rd SO41	19 G5
Kings Yard SP6	11 E3
Kingsbere Gdns BH23	14 D4
Kingsbury La BH24	25 A3
Kingsfield, Lymington SO41	19 G5
Kingsfield, Ringwood BH24	25 C3
Kingsley Cl BH6	12 A6
Kingsley Gdns SO40	26 B5
Kingston Pk SO41	18 D5
Kinross Rd SO40	27 E5
Kitchers Cl SO41	6 B4
Kitwalls La SO41	21 D2
Kivernell Pl*, Kivernell Rd SO41	21 C3
Kivernell Rd SO41	21 C3
Knapp Cl BH23	12 A2
Knapp Mill Av BH23	12 A2
Knellers La SO40	4 C1
Knightcrest Pk SO41	24 C5
Knighton Pk BH25	15 H4
Knightstone Grange SO45	17 F4
Knightwood Av SO43	20 B3
Knightwood Cl, Christchurch BH23	14 B4
Knightwood Cl, Lyndhurst SO43	20 B3
Knightwood Cl, Southampton SO40	4 B3
Knightwood Rd SO45	17 G4
Knowland Dr SO41	21 E2
Knowle Rd SO42	7 B3
Knowles Cl BH23	12 D3
Laburnum Dr SO41	24 B5
Lackford Av SO40	27 E5
Ladycross Rd SO45	17 F5
Ladysmith Cl BH23	12 D3
Lake Grove Rd BH25	22 B3
Lakeside BH24	25 E4
Lakeview Dr BH24	25 E4
Lakewood Rd, Christchurch BH23	14 C3
Lakewood Rd, Southampton SO40	4 B2
Lambourne Cl SO45	17 E5
Lammas Rd SO45	17 G5
Lancaster Rd BH23	13 H3
Lanehays Rd SO45	17 E3
Langdown Firs SO45	17 F4
Langdown Lawn SO45	17 F4
Langdown Lawn Cl SO45	17 F4
Langdown Rd SO45	17 G3
Langley Gdn SP6	11 F2
Langley Lodge Gdns SO45	10 A6
Langley Rd BH23	14 B3
Langton Cl BH25	23 C6
Lapwing Dr SO40	26 B3
Larch Cl SO41	24 A1
Larchwood Rd SO40	26 B5
Lark Rd BH24	13 G5
Larkshill Cl BH25	22 C3
Latch Farm Av BH23	12 A2
Latchmore Dr SO45	16 C3
Latimers Cl BH23	14 C3
Laundry La SO41	21 F3
Laurel Cl, Christchurch BH23	14 A3
Laurel Cl, Lymington SO41	24 A1
Laurel Cl, Southampton SO45	17 E3
Lauren Way SO40	26 A2
Lavender Rd SO41	24 A2
Lawford Way SO40	26 D4
Lawn Cl SO41	21 F3
Lawn Rd, Lymington SO41	18 C4
Lawn Rd, Milford on Sea SO41	21 F3
Lawrence Rd BH24	25 E1
Le Patourel Cl BH23	12 D3
Lea Cl SO43	20 C4
Lebanon Rd SO15	27 H4
Ledbury Rd BH23	13 E5
Leelands SO41	18 D5
Leigh Pk SO41	18 D3
Leigh Rd BH25	22 B3
Lentune Way SO41	19 E5
Lepe Rd SO45	10 A6
Lewis Cl SO45	17 F5
Lexby Rd SO40	27 F6
Leyside BH23	13 F3
Library Rd SO40	27 F4
Lightning Cl SO45	10 B3
Lights Cl BH23	12 A3
Lilac Cl BH24	25 C2
Lime Cl SO45	16 D5
Lime Gro SO41	24 B5
Lime Walk SO45	16 D5
Linbrook Ct BH24	25 B1
Linda Rd SO45	10 C2
Linden Ct*, Linden Gdns BH24	25 A2
Linden Gdns BH24	25 B2
Linden Way SO41	18 C3
Lineside BH23	12 C2
Linford Cl BH25	22 C3
Linford Rd BH24	25 E1
Lingwood Av BH23	13 E4
Linhorns La BH25	22 C1
Link Rd BH24	25 D2
Linnet Cl BH24	25 E4
Linnet Cl BH25	22 A4
Linwood Cl SO45	17 F5
Lisle Cl SO41	19 E4
Lisle Court Rd SO41	19 H3
Litchford Rd BH25	22 D3
Little Barrs Dr BH25	22 C3
Little Burn SO41	6 C4
Little Dene Copse SO41	18 C5
Little Reynolds SO40	26 C6
Livingstone Rd BH23	12 D3
Lockerley Cl SO41	19 E5
Locks Cotts SO45	16 C1
Lodge Dr SO45	17 F5
Lodge Rd SO41	18 C4
Long Beech Dr SO40	26 D5
Longbridge Ct SO40	26 D1
Longbridge Cl SO40	26 C1
Longfield Rd SO41	24 C3
Longford Pl SO41	18 C6
Longleat Gdns BH25	15 H1
Longmead Rd BH24	8 B2

Longmeadow Gdns
  SO45   17 F3
Longstock Cres SO40 26 D4
Loperwood SO40 26 A1
Loperwood La SO40 26 A1
Loraine Av BH23 15 F4
Lovage Gdns SO40 26 B4
Love La SO41 21 E3
Lower Ashley Rd
  BH25 22 E4
Lower Bartons SP6 11 E3
Lower Brownhill Rd
  SO16 27 H2
Lower Buckland Rd
  SO41 18 D1
Lower Mead End Rd
  SO41 6 A6
Lower Mullins La
  SO45 17 E3
Lower Pennington La
  SO41 18 D6
Lucerne Rd SO41 21 E3
Lulworth Bsns Pk
  SO40 26 D1
Lumby Dr BH24 25 D2
Lumby Dr Caravan Pk
  BH24 25 D2
Lunedale Rd SO45 16 D6
Lychgate Ct BH24 25 E4
Lydgate SO40 26 C5
Lydlynch Rd SO40 27 E4
Lyme Cres BH23 14 D5
Lymefields SO41 21 E2
Lymington Rd,
  Brockenhurst SO42 7 D6
Lymington Rd,
  Christchurch BH23 14 B5
Lymington Rd,
  Everton SO41 24 B5
Lymington Rd,
  Lymington SO41 18 A6
Lymington Rd,
  Milford on Sea SO41 21 E2
Lymington Rd,
  New Milton BH25 23 B6
Lymore La,
  Everton SO41 24 B6
Lymore La,
  Milford on Sea SO41 21 F1
Lymore Valley SO41 21 F1
Lyndale Cl SO41 21 E3
Lyndhurst Rd,
  Ashurst SO40 4 A5
Lyndhurst Rd,
  Beaulieu SO42 5 A1
Lyndhurst Rd,
  Brockenhurst SO42 7 D1
Lyndhurst Rd,
  Cadnam SO40 9 B2
Lyndhurst Rd,
  Christchurch BH23 13 G2
Lyndhurst Rd,
  Ringwood BH24 8 E1
Lynes La BH24 25 A3
Lynric Cl BH25 23 B8
Lynton Ct SO40 26 D6
Lyon Av BH23 22 C4
Lysander Cl BH23 13 H3
Lyster Rd SP6 11 F3
Lyteltane Rd SO41 18 D5
Lytton Rd SO45 17 G4

Madeira Walk SO41 19 F3
Magdalen La BH23 12 A4
Magnolia Cl,
  Bournemouth BH6 12 A6
Magnolia Cl,
  Southampton SO45 16 C3
Magpie Dr SO40 26 C4
Magpie Gro BH25 23 A5
Maiden La SO41 19 F6
Main Rd, Hythe SO45 16 C1
Main Rd, Hythe SO45 16 C1
Main Rd,
  Southampton SO40 4 D2
Mallard Cl,
  Christchurch BH23 13 G4
Mallard Cl,
  Lymington SO41 24 C2
Mallory Cl BH23 13 F2
Mallow Cl BH23 13 H2
Malmesbury Cl BH23 12 A5
Malvern Ct*,
  Dorset Rd BH23 13 F2
Malvern Dr SO45 16 D4
Malwood Gdns SO40 26 B4
Malwood Rd SO45 17 E2
Malwood Rd West
  SO45 17 E2

Manchester Rd SO41 6 B4
Manderley SO41 21 E4
Manning Av BH23 14 A3
Manor Cl,
  Lymington SO41 21 D2
Manor Cl,
  Southampton SO40 26 D5
Manor Ct,
  Fordingbridge SP6 11 F3
Manor Ct,
  Ringwood BH24 25 B2
Manor Farm Cl BH25 23 A5
Manor Farm Rd SP6 11 B3
Manor Gdns BH24 25 B3
Manor Rd,
  Christchurch BH23 12 A4
Manor Rd,
  Lymington SO41 21 D2
Manor Rd,
  New Milton BH25 22 C4
Manor Rd,
  Ringwood BH24 25 C3
Manor Rd,
  Southampton SO45 16 A2
Mansell Cl SO45 16 D6
Mansergh Walk SO40 26 A3
Mansfield Rd BH24 25 B3
Maple Cl,
  Christchurch BH23 14 D5
Maple Cl,
  New Milton BH25 23 C8
Maple Gdns SO40 26 B5
Maplewood Cl SO40 26 B5
Marabout Cl BH23 12 D3
Marbream Cl SP6 11 C3
Marchwood By-Pass
  SO40 27 E6
Marine Ct BH25 15 G5
Marine Dr BH25 23 A8
Marine Dr East BH25 23 B8
Marine Dr West BH25 15 G5
Mariners Ct,
  Christchurch BH23 13 F4
Mariners Ct,
  Lymington SO41 19 F4
Mariners Mws SO45 17 G3
Market Pl,
  Fordingbridge SP6 11 E4
Market Pl,
  Ringwood BH24 25 A3
Marks La BH25 22 B1
Marl La BH24 11 B2
Marlborough Ct
  SO45 17 E4
Marlborough Pl SO41 18 D2
Marley Av BH25 22 A3
Marley Cl BH25 22 A4
Marlpit Dr BH23 15 E3
Marmion Grn BH23 13 E3
Marram Cl SO41 19 E1
Marryat Ct,
  Christchurch BH23 15 E5
Marryat Ct,
  New Milton BH25 22 A3
Marryat Rd BH25 22 A4
Marsh Ditch BH23 12 A4
Marsh La,
  Christchurch BH23 12 D4
Marsh La,
  Lymington SO41 19 E1
Marsh La,
  Southampton SO45 10 C1
Marsh Par SO45 17 F2
Marshlands Cl BH23 12 D4
Marston Cl BH25 22 D2
Marston Gro BH23 14 C3
Marston Rd BH25 22 C2
Martins Hill Cl BH23 12 C1
Martins Hill La BH23 12 C1
Martins Rd SO42 7 D2
Mary Mitchell Cl*,
  Kings Arms La BH24 25 A3
Marybridge Cl SO40 26 D6
Maryland Ct SO41 21 B3
Maryland Gdns SO41 21 C3
Masterson Cl BH23 12 D3
Matley Gdns SO40 26 B4
Maturin Cl SO41 19 E4
May Av SO41 19 E2
May Rd BH25 15 E3
Mayfield Av SO40 27 E4
Mayfield Rd SP6 11 B3
Mayflower Cl SO41 19 G4
Mayfly Cl SP6 11 E2
Maynard Rd SO40 27 E4
Meacher Cl SO40 26 D4
Mead End Rd SO41 6 A5
Mead Rd SO41 18 C5
Meadow Av SP6 11 E3

Meadow Cl,
  Burley BH24 8 B4
Meadow Cl,
  Christchurch BH23 6 B3
Meadow Cl,
  Fordingbridge SP6 11 E2
Meadow Cl,
  Ringwood BH24 25 C2
Meadow Cl,
  Southampton SO40 27 E6
Meadow Ct SP6 11 E3
Meadow End SO42 7 B3
Meadow Rd,
  Lymington SO41 18 C5
Meadow Rd,
  New Milton BH25 22 C3
Meadow Rd,
  Ringwood BH24 25 C2
Meadow Way,
  New Milton BH25 23 C8
Meadow Way,
  Ringwood BH24 25 C2
Meadow Way,
  Southampton SO45 10 C2
Meadowland BH23 13 E4
Meadowlands SO41 18 C3
Medina Way BH23 14 A6
Medlar Cl BH23 12 C1
Meerut Rd SO42 7 C3
Meeting House La
  BH24 25 A2
Melbury Cl SO41 18 D3
Melrose Ct,
  New Milton BH25 22 E4
Melrose Ct,
  Southampton SO40 26 B3
Mendip Cl BH25 23 D5
Mendip Ct*,
  Dorset Rd BH23 13 F2
Mendip Gdns SO45 16 D4
Meredith Cl BH23 12 D3
Meredith Gdns SO40 26 C5
Merley Dr BH23 14 D4
Merlin Cl BH24 25 E4
Merlin Way BH25 13 G5
Merriemeade Cl SO45 17 E6
Merriemeade Par
  SO45 17 E6
Merrivale Cl SO45 17 E3
Merryfield Cl BH23 6 B2
Merryweather Est
  BH24 25 E2
Merton Cl SP6 11 E2
Merton Ct BH23 15 E5
Merton Gro BH24 25 A3
Meyrick Cl BH23 6 B3
Michaels Way SO45 17 E2
Michigan Way SO40 26 A3
Middle Common Rd
  SO41 18 A3
Middle La BH24 25 B3
Middle Rd,
  Lymington SO41 18 C6
Middle Rd, Sway SO41 6 B5
Middle Rd,
  Tiptoe SO41 6 A6
Middleton Mews*,
  Chaucombe Pl BH25 23 A6
Middleton Rd BH24 25 C2
Midway BH23 17 E4
Milford Cres SO41 21 E3
Milford Ct SO41 21 E3
Milford Rd,
  Everton SO41 24 B5
Milford Rd,
  Lymington SO41 18 C6
Milford Rd,
  New Milton BH25 23 C6
Milford Trading Est
  SO41 21 E3
Milkwood Ct SO40 26 B4
Mill Ct SP6 11 E4
Mill La,
  Brockenhurst SO42 7 D4
Mill La,
  Lymington SO41 19 F3
Mill La,
  Ringwood BH24 8 E1
Mill Mdw SO41 21 D3
Mill Rd,
  Christchurch BH23 12 A2
Mill Rd,
  Southampton SO40 27 F4
Mill Way SO40 26 D6
Miller Cl BH25 22 D3
Miller Rd BH23 12 D3
Millers Way SO45 17 E5

Millfield BH25 15 H1
Millhams St BH23 12 B4
Millhams St North
  BH23 12 B4
Milliken Cl SO45 10 B3
Millyford Cl BH25 15 G4
Milne Cl SO45 16 C4
Milton Gro BH25 23 C5
Milton Mead BH25 23 A5
Milverton Cl,
  Christchurch BH23 14 C3
Milverton Cl,
  Southampton SO40 27 F6
Milverton Rd SO40 27 F6
Minterne Rd BH23 13 E5
Mitchell Cl BH25 23 B7
Moat La BH25 23 B6
Moffat Rd BH23 12 D3
Molefields SO41 21 E3
Molyneaux Rd BH25 22 E4
Monks Pl SO40 26 D5
Monks Walk SO45 17 E6
Monkshood Cl BH23 13 H1
Monkswell Grn BH23 12 C4
Monkton La SO40 26 C6
Monmouth Gdns
  SO40 26 B6
Montagu Pk BH23 15 E5
Montagu Rd BH23 15 E5
Montague Ct SO45 16 D6
Monteray Dr SO41 24 B1
Montgomery Av
  SO40 26 B6
Monument La SO41 19 G1
Moonrakers Way
  BH23 14 B4
Moore Cl BH25 23 A6
Moorhill Rd BH24 8 C4
Moorland Av BH25 23 A6
Moorland Cl SO45 16 C4
Moorlands Cl SO42 7 A3
Mopley SO45 10 A6
Mopley Cl SO45 10 A5
Morant Rd BH24 25 D1
Morpeth Av SO40 27 E3
Morris Cl SO45 16 C3
Mortimer Cl,
  Christchurch BH23 13 G4
Mortimer Cl,
  Southampton SO40 26 C2
Mount Av BH25 23 C5
Mount Cl BH25 23 C6
Mount House Cl SO45 17 F1
Mount Pleasant Dr
  BH23 6 D1
Mount Pleasant La
  BH24 25 B3
Mountbatten Cl BH23 13 F5
Mountbatten Ct*,
  Raleigh Cl BH25 22 A4
Mountbatten Rd SO40 26 D4
Mountfield SO45 16 D2
Mousehole La SO45 17 F3
Moxhams SP6 11 E3
Mude Gdns BH23 13 F5
Mudeford BH23 13 E5
Mudeford Green Cl
  BH23 13 F5
Mudeford La BH23 12 D4
Mulberry Gdns SP6 11 E4
Mulberry Gro SO41 24 B5
Mussett Cl SO40 26 D4
Myrtle Av SO40 26 C5
Myrtle Cl SO41 24 A1

Nada Rd BH23 14 A3
Naish Est BH25 15 F/G5
Naish Rd BH25 15 H5
Narrow La BH24 25 E1
Nash Cl SO45 16 D5
Nash Rd SO45 16 C5
Nea Cl BH23 14 B4
Nea Rd BH23 14 B5
Neacroft Cl BH23 15 G5
Needles Ct SO41 21 C3
Needles Point SO41 21 D4
Nelson Cl BH23 22 A4
Nelson Cl SO45 17 G5
Nelson Dr BH23 13 F4
Nelson Pl SO41 19 F3
New Cotts SO16 27 H1
New Ct BH24 25 A3
New Forest Dr SO42 7 A2
New Forest Enterprise
  Centre SO40 26 D6
New Inn La SO40 9 D3
New Inn Rd SO40 9 D3
New La,
  Lymington SO41 21 F4

New La,
  New Milton BH25 22 A1
New Rd, Ashurst SO40 4 B3
New Rd, Fawley SO45 10 A4
New Rd,
  Southampton SO45 17 F2
New St,
  Lymington SO41 19 E3
New St,
  Ringwood BH24 25 B4
New St Mws SO41 19 E3
New Valley Rd SO41 21 D3
Newbridge Rd SO40 9 C1
Newbridge Way SO41 18 D6
Newcroft Gdns BH23 12 A2
Newenham Rd SO41 19 E5
Newlands Cl SO45 10 A5
Newlands Copse
  SO45 10 A4
Newlands Rd,
  Christchurch BH23 13 F3
Newlands Rd,
  New Milton BH25 23 C5
Newlands Rd,
  Southampton SO45 10 A3
Newton Rd BH25 23 C6
Nicholas Cl BH23 15 E3
Nicholas Rd SO45 10 A6
Nickleby Gdns SO40 26 B5
Nightingale Dr SO40 26 B3
Noads Cl SO45 17 E6
Noads Way SO45 16 D7
Noel Cl SO42 7 D2
Norleywood BH23 14 C4
Norman Rd SO45 10 A5
Normandy Cl SO41 6 B5
Normandy Dr BH23 12 D2
Normandy La SO41 19 G5
Normandy Way SP6 11 E3
Norris Gdns BH25 23 C5
North Cl SO41 19 F3
North Greenlands
  SO41 18 D6
North Head SO41 21 B4
North Poulner Rd
  BH24 25 C4
North Rd,
  Brockenhurst SO42 7 D1
North Rd,
  Southampton SO45 16 C1
North St SO41 18 C5
North Weirs SO42 7 A1
Northampton La
  SO45 10 A4
Northbourne Cl SO45 17 F1
Northerwood Av
  SO43 20 A4
Northfield Rd,
  Lymington SO41 21 F2
Northfield Rd,
  Ringwood BH24 25 B4
Northlands Cl SO40 26 D4
Northlands Rd SO40 26 D4
Northover Rd SO41 18 B5
Norton Cl BH23 12 D3
Nouale La BH24 25 E4
Nursery Rd BH24 25 E4
Nutsey Av SO40 26 D2
Nutsey Cl SO40 26 D2
Nutsey La SO40 26 D3
Nutshalling Cl SO40 26 B6
Nutwood Way SO40 26 D1

Oak Cl, Hythe SO45 16 D5
Oak Cl,
  Lyndhurst SO43 20 B5
Oak Cl, Totton SO15 27 H3
Oak Ct*,
  Pennington Cl SO41 18 C5
Oak Gdns SO41 24 B5
Oak La BH24 25 C4
Oak Rd,
  New Milton BH25 22 D3
Oak Rd,
  Southampton SO40 16 D1
Oak Tree Par BH23 6 C2
Oakdene SO40 26 B5
Oakenbrow,
  Lymington SO41 6 A4
Oakenbrow,
  Southampton SO45 16 D6
Oakfield Rd,
  Cadnam SO40 9 B1
Oakfield Rd,
  Totton SO40 26 D5
Oaklands SO41 19 F3
Oaklands Av SO40 27 G5
Oaklands Cl SP6 11 E4
Oaklands Way SO45 16 D6

leigh Cres SO40 26 D5
leigh Way BH23 14 C5
mount Av SO40 27 E4
ridge Rd SO15 27 F3
tree Ct SO41 21 C3
wood Av BH25 22 D3
wood Ct BH25 22 C4
wood Rd BH23 14 C3
field Gdns SO40 26 C2
er Rd SO42 7 B3
rfield Rd SO42 7 A2
nell Gro SO45 16 C3
Barn Cl BH24 25 D3
Brickyard Rd SP6 11 A2
Christchurch Rd
041 24 A5
Farm Walk SO41 19 E4
Farmhouse Mws
041 19 E2
Lyndhurst Rd
040 9 B2
Mill Ho BH24 25 A4
Milton Grn BH25 23 A6
Milton Rd BH25 23 B6
Orchs SO41 19 F5
Redbridge Rd
015 27 H3
Romsey Rd SO40 9 A2
Stacks Gdns
24 25 D4
Vicarage La SO41 6 C6
barn Cl SO40 26 B1
er Rd SO41 18 C4
ers Cl SO40 26 A5
hard Cl,
ristchurch BH23 12 A4
hard Cl,
wley SO45 10 C2
hard Cl,
rdingbridge SP6 11 E2
hard Rd,
mington SO41 21 D2
ngwood BH24 25 B2
uthampton SO40 27 E6
hard Gdns SP6 11 E4
hard Gro BH25 23 B6
hard Mead BH24 25 B2
hard Mt BH24 25 B3
hard Mws BH23 12 A4
hard Way SO45 17 E4
hid Way SO41 12 C3
orne Ct SO41 21 C3
orne Rd,
w Milton BH25 22 C4
orne Rd,
uthampton SO40 27 F5
rey Cl BH23 13 F5
ers Walk BH25 22 D1
rbrook SO45 17 E4
rstrand Cres SO41 21 E4
at Cl SO40 26 B4
ey Cl BH25 23 B6
ord Ter SO41 6 C4
ddock Gdns SO41 18 D2
get Rd BH24 25 E1
stow Pl SP6 11 D4
ace La SO42 5 C4
ner Pl BH25 22 C3
merston Av BH23 12 D4
plyn Cl SO41 18 D2
adise La SO40 9 F4
ham Cl BH25 22 A4
x Av SO40 18 D2
x Cl,
ockenhurst SO42 7 C2
x Cl,
mington SO41 21 E3
x Cl,
ndhurst SO43 20 C6
x Cl,
w Milton BH25 22 D2
uthampton SO45 17 G3
x Ct SO41 21 D3
x Gdns BH23 13 E4
x La SO41 21 D4
x Rd,
rton on Sea BH25 22 D2
x Rd,
rdingbridge SP6 11 E3
x Rd,
mington SO41 18 D2
x Rd,
ilford on Sea SO41 21 E4
x Rd,
w Milton BH25 23 A6

Park Vw BH25 22 B4
Parkers Cl BH24 25 E2
Parkland Dr BH25 23 A6
Parklands SO40 27 F3
Parkside,
Christchurch BH23 14 B3
Parkside,
Ringwood BH24 25 B4
Parkside,
Southampton SO40 27 E6
Parsonage Barn La
BH24 25 D4
Parsonage Cl SP6 11 E3
Parsonage Park Dr SP6 11 E2
Partridge Cl BH23 13 F5
Partridge Grn BH25 22 D1
Partridge Rd,
Brockenhurst SO42 7 C4
Partridge Rd,
Southampton SO45 17 F5
Pat Bear Cl SO15 27 H4
Pauletts La SO40 26 B1
Pauntley Rd BH23 13 E4
Peace Cl BH23 6 B2
Pealsham Gdns SP6 11 D2
Pear Tree Cl BH23 6 C2
Pearce Smith Ct BH25 23 A8
Pearmain Dr SO41 19 F5
Peartree Cl SO41 19 F5
Peartree Rd SO45 17 E4
Peckham Av BH25 22 B4
Pedlars Walk BH24 25 A3
Pegasus Av SO41 24 C3
Pelham Cl BH23 12 D4
Pelican Mead BH24 25 E4
Pemberton Rd SO43 20 C3
Pembridge Rd SP6 11 F2
Pembroke Cl SO40 27 F3
Pembroke Dr BH23 15 E5
Pendleton Gdns SO45 10 A4
Penelope Ct BH23 15 E5
Penhale Way SO40 26 D6
Penn Cl BH23 23 A6
Pennant Way BH23 13 F3
Pennine Ct*,
Hunt Rd BH23 13 F2
Pennine Gdns SO45 16 C4
Pennington Cl SO41 18 C5
Pennington Oval
SO41 18 B4
Penny Hedge BH25 23 C7
Penny Way BH23 14 A6
Pennys Cl SP6 11 E2
Pennys Cres SP6 11 E2
Pennys La SP6 11 E2
Pennywell Gdns
BH25 22 E3
Pentland Cl SO40 16 C5
Pentridge Way SO40 26 D6
Percy Cl SO45 17 E1
Peregrine Cl SO40 26 C5
Peregrine Rd BH23 13 F5
Perrywood Gdns
SO40 26 B3
Peterscroft Av SO40 4 A4
Picket Cl SP6 11 E3
Pickwick Cl SO40 26 A5
Pikes Cl BH24 25 D2
Pikes Hill SO43 20 A2
Pikes Hill Av SO43 20 B2
Pilgrim Pk Homes
Caravan Pk BH24 25 D2
Pilgrim Pl SO41 19 E4
Pilgrims Cl BH25 22 D3
Pine Cl, Hythe SO45 17 E5
Pine Cl,
New Milton BH25 15 H5
Pine Cl,
Southampton SO40 4 B2
Pine Cres BH23 14 C5
Pinecliffe Rd BH25 15 G5
Pinehurst Av BH23 13 F5
Pinetops Cl SO41 18 B3
Pinewood Cl BH23 14 D3
Pinewood Cres SO45 17 G5
Pinewood Dr SO45 17 G5
Pinewood Rd,
Christchurch BH23 14 D3
Pinewood Rd,
Lymington SO41 24 A2
Pinkney La SO43 20 A6
Pipers Ash BH24 25 E2
Pipers Cl SO40 26 D5
Pipers Dr BH23 13 G3
Pippin Cl SO41 19 F5
Pitts Pl BH25 22 F4
Plantation Cl SO41 6 B5
Plantation Dr BH23 15 E2
Player Cl SP6 11 F2

Players Cres SO40 27 E6
Pleasance Way BH25 22 A4
Pless Rd SO41 21 B3
Plover Dr SO41 21 F4
Plover Rd SO40 26 C4
Poles La SO41 19 E6
Pollards Moor Rd
SO40 9 D1
Pond Cl BH25 22 B4
Popes La SO40 27 E4
Poplar Cl,
Bransgore BH23 6 D2
Poplar Cl,
Christchurch BH23 15 E4
Poplar Cres BH24 25 D3
Poplar La BH23 6 C2
Poplar Rd BH25 22 E3
Poplar Way BH24 25 D3
Poppy Cl BH23 13 H2
Porlock Rd SO16 27 H2
Portal Rd SO40 26 D4
Portfield Cl BH23 12 A2
Poulner Hill BH24 25 F2
Poulner Pk BH24 25 E1
Pound Cl BH24 25 B2
Pound La,
Ashurst SO40 9 E1
Pound La,
Cadnam SO40 4 D2
Pound La,
Ringwood BH24 8 A4
Pound Rd SO41 18 C4
Powell Cres SO40 27 E6
Powers Court Rd
BH25 15 H5
Powis Cl BH25 22 E4
Powlett Rd SO41 19 E4
Preston Way BH23 14 A5
Prestwood Cl BH25 23 A6
Priestlands La SO41 18 D4
Priestlands Pl SO41 19 E4
Priestlands Rd SO41 18 D4
Priestley Cl SO40 26 C5
Primrose Way BH23 13 H2
Princes Cres SO43 20 D3
Princes Pl BH25 22 D3
Princess Av BH23 12 B5
Princess Rd SO40 14 A4
Priors Cl BH23 14 A6
Priory Ct BH23 12 B5
Priory Ind Pk BH23 13 G3
Priory Quay BH23 13 H5
Private Rd SO41 19 F2
Promenade BH23 13 H5
Prospect Pl SO45 17 E5
Provost St SP6 11 E4
Puddletown La SP6 11 C2
Pullman Way BH24 25 C4
Pundle Grn SO40 9 E4
Purbeck Ct*,
Dorset Rd BH23 13 F2
Purbeck Rd BH25 15 G5
Purewell BH23 12 D4
Purewell Cl BH23 12 D4
Purewell Cross Rd
BH23 12 C3
Purewell Ct BH23 12 D3
Pylewell Rd SO45 17 F2
Pyrford Mws SO41 19 E5

Quantock Ct*,
Hunt Rd BH23 13 F2
Quarr Ho SO41 6 B4
Quay Rd BH23 12 B4
Quay St SO41 19 F3
Queen Elizabeth Av
SO41 18 D3
Queen Katherine Rd
SO41 19 F3
Queen St SO41 19 F3
Queens Av BH23 12 B5
Queens Cl SO45 17 G4
Queens Ct BH25 22 E3
Queens Gdns SP6 11 E2
Queens Gro BH25 22 E3
Queens Par SO43 20 C3
Queens Rd,
Christchurch BH23 12 D4
Queens Rd,
Lyndhurst SO43 20 D3
Queens Way BH24 25 C3
Queensway SO41 15 H2
Quinton Cl BH23 13 E4
Quomp BH24 25 B3

Raleigh Cl,
Christchurch BH23 13 F5
Raleigh Cl,
New Milton BH25 22 A4
Raleigh Cl,
Ringwood BH24 25 E2
Ramley Rd SO41 18 A1
Ramsey Ct BH25 22 A4
Randall Cl SO40 26 C1
Randalls La BH24 8 A1
Ranelagh Rd BH23 14 C5
Ranfurly Gdns SO45 17 E5
Ranmore Ct SO45 16 B3
Ratcliffe Rd SO45 17 F5
Raven Way BH23 13 F5
Ravens Croft Rd SO41 18 D1
Ravens Way SO41 21 D4
Ravenscourt Rd SO41 19 E4
Redan Cl BH23 14 D5
Redbridge Causeway
SO40 27 G4
Redbridge Flyover
SO16 27 H3
Redbridge La,
Southampton SO16 27 G3
Redbridge La,
Southampton SO16 27 H2
Redbridge La,
Redbridge Rd SO15 27 H3
Redbridge Towers
SO16 27 H3
Redvers Cl SO41 19 F4
Redvers Rd BH23 12 D3
Redwing Gdns SO40 26 B3
Redwood Cl,
Lymington SO41 18 D2
Redwood Cl,
Ringwood BH24 25 C3
Redwood Cl,
Southampton SO45 16 C4
Redwood Gdns SO40 26 B3
Reeder Cl SP6 11 D4
Regency Pl BH24 25 B2
Regent Way BH23 12 B4
Reid St BH23 12 D3
Renouf Cl SO41 18 C4
Reynolds Dale SO40 4 C1
Rhinefield Cl SO42 7 B3
Rhinefield Rd SO42 7 A3
Rhiners Cl SO41 6 B4
Rhyme Hall Mws
SO45 10 D2
Ricardo Cres BH23 13 G4
Richards Cl SO45 10 B3
Richmond Cl SO40 26 B2
Richmond Ct SO41 21 D4
Ridgefield Gdns BH23 14 B4
Ridgeway La SO41 18 D5
Ridgewood Cl SO45 16 B3
Rimbury Way BH23 12 A2
Ringbury SO41 19 E1
Ringwood By-Pass
BH24 25 A3
Ringwood Rd,
Bransgore BH23 6 B1
Ringwood Rd,
Cadnam SO40 9 F3
Ringwood Rd,
Christchurch BH23 14 C1
Ringwood Rd,
Ringwood BH24 8 A1
Ringwood Rd,
Southampton SO40 26 A5
Ringwood Trading Est
BH25 25 C4
River Ct SO41 19 F2
River Gdns SO41 21 E3
Riverdale Cl SP6 11 E2
Riverdale La BH23 12 A4
Riverlea Rd BH23 12 A4
Riversdale Rd BH6 12 A4
Riverside BH24 25 A4
Riverside Cl SO45 9 E4
Riverside Pk BH23 12 A4
Riverside Pl SO41 19 F3
Roberts Cl SO41 24 B5
Roberts Rd,
Hythe SO45 17 E2
Roberts Rd,
Southampton SO40 27 E6
Robin Gdns,
Christchurch BH23 12 A3
Robin Gdns,
Southampton SO40 26 B3
Robin Gro BH25 23 A5
Robins Way BH23 13 G5
Rockbourne Gdns
BH25 15 G5
Rockery Cl SO45 16 C3
Rockleigh Dr SO40 4 D1

Rockram Cl SO40 9 D3
Rockram Gdns SO45 16 B3
Rodbourne Cl SO41 24 A5
Rodney Cl BH23 13 F4
Rodney Dr BH23 13 F4
Roebuck Cl BH25 22 D4
Roeshot Cres BH23 14 B3
Roeshot Hill BH23 13 H1
Roman Cl SO45 16 C5
Roman Quay SP6 11 E4
Roman Rd SO45 16 C5
Roman Way SO45 16 C5
Romsey Rd,
Lyndhurst SO43 20 B1
Romsey Rd,
Southampton SO40 9 B2
Rook Hill Rd BH23 13 H5
Rookcliff Way SO41 21 C3
Rookes La SO41 19 E5
Rooksbridge SO45 16 B3
Roscrea Cl BH6 12 B6
Roscrea Dr BH6 12 B6
Rose Cl SO45 17 F5
Rose Rd SO40 27 F5
Rosebery Av SO40 17 G5
Rosecrae Cl BH25 22 A3
Rosedale Cl BH23 13 E4
Rosehill Cl BH23 6 C1
Rosehill Dr BH23 6 B2
Roseleigh Dr SO40 26 D6
Rosemary Ct,
Christchurch BH23 15 E5
Rosemary Ct,
Southampton SO40 26 B4
Rosewood Gdns
BH25 22 A3
Ross Rd BH24 25 E1
Rossiters Quay BH23 12 C4
Rossley Cl BH23 14 C3
Rothbury Cl SO40 26 C2
Rothbury Pk BH25 22 D4
Rotherfield Rd BH23 14 D3
Rothesay Dr BH23 14 C5
Rotterdam Dr BH23 12 C4
Round Copse SO45 16 B3
Round Hill BH25 11 E3
Roundhouse Dr SO40 26 B5
Rowan Cl,
Christchurch BH23 14 B4
Rowan Cl,
Lymington SO41 6 B6
Rowan Cl,
Southampton SO40 26 C6
Rowan Dr BH23 14 A4
Rowans Pk SO41 18 D4
Rowhill Dr SO45 16 B3
Royston Pl BH25 23 C7
Rubens Cl BH25 22 D4
Ruby Cl SO40 26 C4
Rufus Cl SO43 20 C4
Rufus Gdns SO40 26 B4
Rumbridge Gdns
SO40 27 F5
Rumbridge St SO40 27 F5
Rushford Warren
BH23 13 F6
Rushington Av SO40 27 E5
Rushington Bsns Pk
SO40 26 D6
Rushington La SO40 26 D6
Rushpole Ct SO45 16 B3
Russell Ct BH25 22 B4
Russell Dr BH23 12 D4
Russet Cl SO41 19 F4
Rye Dale SO40 4 B2
Rye Paddock La SO45 10 D1
Sadlers La SO45 17 F5
Saffron Dr BH23 13 H2
St Annes Gdns SO41 18 D4
St Davids Cl SO40 26 B2
St Denys*,
Station Rd BH25 23 C5
St Francis Cl SO40 10 A6
St Francis Rd SO40 10 A6
St Georges Cl,
Bransgore BH23 6 C2
St Georges Cl,
Christchurch BH23 14 B5
St Georges Cres SP6 11 E2
St Georges Rd SP6 11 E2
St James Rd SO41 6 C5
St Johns St SO45 17 G2
St Margarets Av BH23 12 A5
St Marks Rd SO41 18 D4
St Mary Gro SO41 24 C3
St Marys Cl BH23 12 A5
St Michaels Cl SO45 10 A4
St Michaels Rd SO40 27 E5

St Thomas Pk SO41 19 E3
St Thomas's St SO41 19 E3
Salcombe Cres SO40 26 D5
Salcombe Rd SO40 26 D5
Salisbury Rd,
Christchurch BH23 12 D1
Salisbury Rd,
Fordingbridge SP6 11 F3
Salisbury Rd,
Ringwood BH24 25 B2
Salisbury Rd,
Southampton SO40 26 C1
Salisbury Road Arc
SO40 27 E4
Salisbury St SP6 11 F3
Salterns La SO45 10 C1
Samber Cl SO41 18 D2
Samphire Cl SO41 19 E1
Sanderlings BH24 25 E4
Sandilands Way SO45 17 G5
Sandle Copse SP6 11 B3
Sandleheath Rd SP6 11 A2
Sandlewood Cl SO40 26 C3
Sandmartin BH25 23 A8
Sandown Rd BH23 13 E4
Sandy La SO43 20 B4
Sandy Plot BH23 12 C1
Saracen Cl SO41 18 D6
Sarah Sands Cl BH23 12 D2
Sarum Walk SO41 18 D1
Saulfland Dr BH23 14 A4
Saulfland Pl BH23 14 A4
Saxon Centre BH23 12 B4
Saxon Pl SO41 10 A5
Saxon Rd SO45 10 A5
Saxon Sq SO41
Saxonford Rd BH23 14 A6
School La,
Lymington SO41 19 E3
School La,
Milford on Sea SO41 21 E2
School La,
Ringwood BH24 25 B3
School Rd,
Fawley SO45 10 C2
School Rd,
Hythe SO45 17 F2
School Rd,
Totton SO40 27 F5
Scott-Paine Dr SO45 17 G2
Scotts Grn BH23 13 F2
Scotts Hills La BH23 12 D4
Sea Rd,
Lymington SO41 21 E4
Sea Rd,
New Milton BH25 15 H4
Sea View Rd BH25 15 G5
Sea Vixen Ind Est
BH23 13 F7
Sea Winds SO41 21 B3
Seacroft Av BH25 15 H5
Seafield Cl BH25 23 A7
Seafield Rd,
Christchurch BH23 13 H4
Seafield Rd,
New Milton BH25 15 H5
Seaton Cl,
Christchurch BH23 15 E4
Seaton Cl,
Lymington SO41 19 E1
Seaton Rd BH23 15 E4
Seaview Rd BH23 15 F3
Seaward Av BH25 15 H5
Seaward Rd SO45 17 G3
Seaway BH25 23 D7
Seaway Av BH23 13 H3
Second Marine Av
BH25 23 B8
Second St SO45 10 B2
Sedgefield Cl SO40 26 C3
Selborne Rd SO40 26 D3
Sellwood Way BH25 15 G4
Selman Cl SO45 17 G2
Serle Cl SO40 26 B4
Serle Gdns SO40 26 D5
Set Thorns Rd SO41 6 C5
Seventh St SO45 10 A1
Seymour Cl SO40 26 C2
Seymour Rd BH23 25 C1
Shackleton Sq BH23 6 C1
Shaftesbury St SP6 11 E4
Shaggs Mdw SO43 20 C4
Shakespeare Dr SO40 26 C2
Shamrock Way SO45 17 F1
Shappen Hill La BH24 20 B4
Sharpley Cl SP6 11 D2
Sharvells Rd SO41 21 C3
Shaves Cl BH25 22 C2
Shaw Cl SO40 26 C4

Shaw Rd BH24 25 E1
Shawford Cl SO40 26 A4
Shears Brook Cl BH23 6 C1
Sheldrake Gdns SO41 24 C2
Sheldrake Rd BH23 13 G5
Shelley Cl BH23 14 A5
Shelley Hill BH23 14 A5
Shelley Rd SO40 26 C2
Shelley Way SO41 21 E3
Shenstone Ct BH25 23 B5
Shepherd Cl BH23 14 C3
Shepherds Cl SO40 9 E4
Shepherds Hey Rd
SO40 26 B2
Shepherds Rd SO40 9 E3
Shepherds Way SO41 24 A5
Sheridan Gdns SO41 26 C5
Sherringham Cl SO45 10 D2
Shetland Cl SO40 26 B3
Shinglebank Dr SO41 21 D3
Shires Walk SO40 26 B4
Shirley Cl BH23 6 C1
Shoblands Way SO45 17 G5
Shore Cl SO41 21 E4
Shore Rd SO45 17 G2
Shorefield Cres SO41 21 C2
Shorefield Rd SO41 21 A1
Shorefield Way SO41 21 C2
Shorts Cl BH23 12 C1
Shraveshill Cl SO40 26 C2
Shrubbs Av SO41 19 E2
Shrubbs Hill Gdns
SO43 20 B4
Shrubbs Hilll Rd
SO43 20 B4
Sidlie Gdns SO40 26 C5
Silver Bsns Pk BH23 13 E3
Silver St,
Christchurch BH23 12 B4
Silver St,
Lymington SO41 24 A1
Silver St,
Lyndhurst SO43 20 A3
Silver Way BH23 14 C5
Silverdale BH25 23 C7
Silvers End SO45 17 F5
Silvers Wood SO40 26 B2
Singleton Way SO40 26 B3
Sir Christopher Cl
SO45 17 G2
Sizer Way SO40 16 B3
Sky End La SO41 24 C3
Slade Cl SO41 24 B2
Slades Hill SO45 10 B3
Slater Cl SO40 26 B3
Slinn Rd BH23 13 E3
Sloe Cl SO41 18 D5
Smith Cl SO45 10 B3
Smithy La BH23 22 A1
Smugglers La North
BH23 14 B3
Smugglers La South
BH23 14 B4
Smugglers Reach
BH23 13 F5
Smugglers Wood Rd
BH23 14 A3
Snellgrove Cl SO40 26 B1
Snooks La SO41 19 H1
Snowdrop Gdns
BH23 13 H2
Solent Av SO41 19 G4
Solent Cl SO41 19 G4
Solent Cl SO41 21 C3
Solent Dr,
New Milton BH25 23 B7
Solent Dr,
Southampton SO45 17 E3
Solent Pines SO41 21 B3
Solent Rd,
Christchurch BH23 15 F3
Solent Rd,
New Milton BH25 15 G5
Solent Rd,
Southampton SO45 17 E6
Solent Way SO41 21 F3
Somerford Av BH23 13 G2
Somerford Bsns Pk
BH23 13 F3
Somerford Rd BH23 13 F4
Somerford Way BH23 13 G4
Somerley Vw BH24 25 B2
Somerton Cl BH23 22 E4
Somerville Ct*,
Marryat Rd BH25 23 A4
Somerville Rd BH24 25 E2
Sopers La BH23 12 A5
Sopley Cl BH25 15 G5
Sopwith Cl BH23 13 G4

Sorrell Ct BH23 13 G2
Sorrell Way BH23 13 G2
South Av,
New Milton BH25 23 C5
South Av,
Southampton SO45 10 A2
South Baddesley Rd
SO41 19 H3
South Gro SO41 19 F4
South Hampshire
Ind Pk SO40 26 D1
South Lawns Walk
BH25 23 A6
South St,
Lymington SO41 18 C4
South St,
Southampton SO45 17 F4
South Sway La SO41 6 C6
South View Rd BH23 12 A4
South Weirs SO42 7 A4
Southampton Rd,
Cadnam SO40 9 A/B2
Southampton Rd,
Fordingbridge SP6 11 F4
Southampton Rd,
Hythe SO45 16 D2
Southampton Rd,
Lymington SO41 18 D1
Southampton Rd,
Lyndhurst SO43 20 C4
Southampton Rd,
Ringwood BH24 25 B3
Southbourne Rd SO41 18 C4
Southcliffe Rd,
Christchurch BH23 13 H4
Southcliffe Rd,
New Milton BH25 15 G5
Southdown Ct*,
Dorset Rd BH23 13 F2
Southern Gdns SO40 26 D4
Southern La BH25 23 A6
Southern Oaks BH25 23 A6
Southern Rd SO41 18 D3
Southey Rd BH23 13 E2
Southfield BH24 25 B4
Southfield La BH24 8 F3
Southfield Mws BH24 25 B4
Southlands SO41 18 C5
Southwood Av BH23 13 G3
Southwood Cl BH23 15 E3
Sovereign Cl SO40 26 B3
Spartina Dr SO41 19 E1
Speedwell Dr BH23 13 G2
Spencer Rd BH25 22 C4
Spicers Hill SO40 27 E6
Spicers Way SO40 27 E6
Spinacre BH25 23 C7
Spindlewood Cl BH25 23 B6
Spinney Dale SO45 17 G5
Spinney Gdns SO45 17 G5
Spinney Way BH25 22 C1
Spittlefields BH24 25 D3
Spring La BH25 23 E5
Spring Rd,
Lymington SO41 19 G4
Spring Rd,
Southampton SO45 17 G3
Springfield Cl SO41 19 G3
Springfield Cl SO40 26 D6
Springfield Gdns
BH25 22 E4
Springwater Dr BH23 12 D4
Spruce Dr SO40 26 A3
Squirrels Walk SO45 17 E5
Stag Cl BH23 22 A3
Stallards La BH24 25 A3
Stanford Rise SO41 6 B5
Stanley Cl,
Christchurch BH23 15 E4
Stanley Rd,
Lymington SO41 19 G5
Stanley Rd,
Southampton SO40 26 D2
Stannington Cl BH23 23 C5
Stannington Cres
SO40 27 E3
Stannington Way
SO40 27 F3
Stanpit BH23 12 D4
Staplecross La BH23 12 D2
Star La BH24 25 A3
Station Rd,
Christchurch BH23 12 A3
Station Rd,
Fordingbridge SP6 11 C3
Station Rd,
Hinton BH23 14 C2
Station Rd,
Lymington SO41 6 B5

Station Rd,
New Milton BH25 22 B4
Station Rd,
Ringwood BH24 8 F4
Station Rd,
Southampton SO15 27 H4
Station Rd North
SO40 27 G4
Station Rd South
SO40 27 G4
Station St SO41 19 F3
Stella Ct BH23 15 E5
Stem La BH25 15 H2
Stephen Martin Gdns
SP6 11 D3
Stephens Walk*,
Kings Arms La BH24 25 A3
Stephenson Rd SO40 26 C1
Stibbs Way BH23 6 D1
Stirling Cl,
New Milton BH25 22 D4
Stirling Cl,
Southampton SO40 27 F3
Stirling Cres SO40 27 F3
Stirling Way BH23 13 G4
Stocklands SO40 26 B1
Stonechat Ct BH23 13 E3
Stonechat Dr SO40 26 B3
Stonehills SO45 10 D3
Stoneleigh Av SO41 24 A1
Stony La BH23 12 C1
Stony La South BH23 12 C4
Stopples La SO41 24 A1
Stour Rd BH23 12 A5
Stourbank Rd BH23 12 A4
Stouts La BH23 6 C2
Stratfield Pl BH23 22 A4
Stratford Pl SO41 18 D2
Strete Mt BH23 13 E3
Strides La BH25 23 A3
Strides Way SO40 26 B5
Stroud Gdns BH23 13 E4
Stroud La BH23 13 E4
Stroud Park Av BH23 13 E4
Stuart Rd BH23 15 E5
Stuckton Rd SP6 11 F4
Studland Dr SO41 21 C3
Studley Cl BH23 15 F4
Studley Cl BH25 15 G4
Summers La BH23 12 D1
Summertrees Ct
BH25 22 E3
Sunderland Dr BH23 13 H3
Sundew Cl,
Christchurch BH23 13 H1
Sundew Cl,
New Milton BH25 22 F3
Sunningdale SO45 17 E4
Sunny Way SO40 27 E4
Sunnyfield Rd BH25 23 B7
Sunset Cl SO40 27 E3
Sunset Rd SO40 27 E4
Surrey Cl SO40 26 D6
Sutton Pl SO42 7 D3
Sutton Rd SO40 26 D2
Swallow Cl SO40 26 B5
Swallow Dr SO41 21 F4
Swan Grn BH23 12 A5
Swan Mead BH24 25 E4
Sway Pk Ind Est
SO41 6 B6
Sway Rd,
Brockenhurst SO42 7 C6
Sway Rd,
Lymington SO41 18 A1
Sway Rd,
New Milton BH25 22 B1
Swordfish Dr BH23 13 G3
Sycamore Cl SO41 21 D2
Sycamore Rd,
Lymington SO41 24 A1
Sycamore Rd,
Southampton SO45 17 E3
Sylvan Cl SO41 24 C3
Sylvia Cres SO40 26 D2

Talbot Dr BH23 14 D3
Talbot Rd SO45 16 D6
Tamar Gro SO45 16 D3
Tamorisk Dr SO40 26 B5
Tangmere Cl BH23 13 G4
Tate Mdws*,
Tate Rd SO15 27 H4
Tate Rd SO15 27 H4
Tates Rd SO45 17 G4
Tattenham Rd SO42 7 C4
Teak Ct SO41 22 E2
Teal Cl SO40 26 C4
Tebourba Cotts SO41 6 C6

Tedder Way SO40 26 C4
Tennyson Rd SO40 26 C2
Tensing Rd BH23 12 D2
Tern Cl SO45 17 H5
Terrington Av BH23 14 B3
Test La SO16 27 G1/3
Test Valley Bsns Centre
SO16 27 G1
Testbourne Av SO40 26 D4
Testbourne Cl SO40 26 C5
Testbourne Rd SO40 26 D2
Testwood Av SO40 26 D2
Testwood Cres SO40 26 C3
Testwood La SO40 27 E3
Testwood Pl SO40 27 F3
The Barracks BH24 8 B
The Bartons SP6 11 E3
The Boltons SO41 21 D4
The Brackens SO45 16 D4
The Bramblings SO40 26 B4
The Brickyard SO40 9 E4
The Bridges BH24 25 A2
The Bucklers SO41 21 B2
The Buttery BH23 12 D
The Cleeves SO40 26 C5
The Cloisters,
Lymington SO41 19 E
The Cloisters,
Ringwood BH24 25 E4
The Close,
Lymington SO41 6 B
The Close,
New Milton BH25 23 C
The Close,
Ringwood BH24 25 B
The Coppice,
Brockenhurst SO42 7 A
The Coppice,
Christchurch BH23 13 G
The Crescent BH25 15 G
The Croft SO40 26 C
The Cross BH24 8 C
The Cul De Sac BH25 15 G
The Custards SO43 20 C
The Dell BH25 15 F
The Dorrits SO40 26 B
The Drive SO40 27 E
The Drove SO40 27 E
The Fairway BH25 23 C
The Fallows BH25 23 C
The Fowey SO45 10 A
The Furlong BH24 24 B
The Grange SO41 24 B
The Green SO41 21 E
The Hawthorns BH23 11 E
The Hundred SP6 11 E
The Hyde BH25 22 A
The Lane SO45 10 D
The Lanes BH25 22 C
The Lawns BH23 15 E
The Linnets SO40 26 B
The Lydgate SO41 21 E
The Mall BH24 8 C
The Mallows BH25 22 B
The Marsh SO45 17 H
The Martells BH25 23 H
The Mead SO45 17 H
The Meadow BH25 15 H
The Meadows SO43 14 D
The Meadway BH23 14 D
The Mews*,
Lepe Rd BH25 10 A
The Mount BH24 25 A
The Old Vineries SP6 11 E
The Orchard,
Christchurch BH23 6 E
The Orchard,
Lymington SO41 21 E
The Paddock,
Brockenhurst SO42 7 E
The Paddock,
Southampton SO40 26 E
The Paddocks SO40 10 E
The Pantiles SP6 11 E
The Parade,
Barton on Sea BH25 23 E
The Parade,
New Milton BH25 22 E
The Parade,
Southampton SO40 9 E
The Park BH25 26 E
The Pentagon SO45 17 E
The Promenade SO45 17 F
The Quadrant*,
Brook Ter SP6 11 E
The Quantocks SO45 16 E
The Rampart SO41 19 E
The Redfords SO40 26 E
The Rise SO42 7 E

The Runway BH23 13 H3
The Spinney SO40 26 B2
The Square,
Lymington SO41 18 C4
The Square,
Southampton SO45 10 D2
The Sweep BH23 25 B3
The Sylvans SO45 16 C4
The Tins SO41 19 E3
The Triangle*,
Naish Est BH25 15 F5
The Vale SO45 17 E4
The Vinery BH25 22 D4
The Wicket SO45 17 E4
The Willows BH25 23 C7
Thetchers Cl BH25 22 C2
Third St SO45 10 B1
Thistle Cl BH23 13 H2
Thomas Cl SO40 26 C5
Thoresby Ct BH25 15 H1
Thornbury Av SO45 10 A5
Thornbury Rd BH6 12 A6
Thorness Cl SO16 27 H2
Thornfield Dr BH23 14 C3
Thornham Rd BH25 22 E4
Thornhill Cl SO45 10 A3
Thornhill Rd SO45 10 A3
Three Acre Cl BH25 23 A6
Three Acre Dr BH25 23 A6
Thursby Rd BH23 14 C3
Tidemill Cl BH23 12 A2
Tiffany Cl SO41 24 B1
Tilburg Rd BH23 12 C4
Tilebarn La SO42 7 C6
Timbermill Ct SP6 11 E4
Timson Cl SO40 26 C5
The Barn SO41 19 E2
Tomer Cl SO45 10 B3
Top La BH24 25 B3
Tormead SO45 17 E4
Totland Ct SO41 21 C3
Totton Western By-Pass
SO40 26 A3
Tracey Ct BH23 14 D5
Trafalgar Cl BH23 13 F5
Trafalgar Pl SO41 19 F3
Trafalgar Way SO45 17 G5
Tranmere Cl SO41 19 F5
Treagore Rd SO40 26 C2
Treebys Cl BH23 12 D1
Treeside BH23 14 A3
Treeside Av SO40 27 F5
Trefoil Way BH23 13 H2
Tresillian Cl BH23 15 E3
Tresillian Way BH23 15 E3
Trevone Cl SO40 26 D6
Trinity Ct SO40 27 E1
Tritoak Cl BH23 12 D2
Trucks Cl SO40 6 B2
Tudor Cl SO40 26 B3
Turners Farm Cres
SO41 24 C3
Twynham Av BH23 12 A4
Tylers Cl SO41 19 E2
Tyrrells Ct BH23 6 C1
Tyrrells La BH24 8 B1

Tytherley Cl BH23 22 B3
Uddershore SO41 19 F1
Undershore Rd SO41 19 F2
Uplands Av BH23 23 C7
Upper Common Rd
SO41 18 A3
Upper Gordon Rd
BH23 15 E4
Upper Mullins La
SO45 17 E3

Veals La SO41 24 A1
Vardant Way BH23 13 G3
Verley Cl SO45 10 A4
Verley Rd SO40 27 E6
Verwydene SO45 17 F5
Vaughan Rd SO45 16 C3
Vecta Cl BH23 13 H2
Vectis Rd BH25 15 G5
Venn Cl SO16 27 H2
Vereheda Ct SO45 17 F1
Violet Lawn Rd BH25 22 A3
Vernalls Ct BH25 22 E2
Viro La BH23 14 A3

Verwood Cres BH6 12 A6
Vetch Cl BH23 13 H2
Vian Ct BH25 22 B4
Vicarage Gdns SO41 24 B3
Vicarage La,
Lymington SO41 24 B2
Vicarage La,
Southampton SO40 9 D1
Vickery Way BH23 12 D3
Victoria Gdns,
Fordingbridge SP6 11 C4
Victoria Gdns,
Ringwood BH24 25 C4
Victoria Pl SO41 19 F4
Victoria Rd,
Christchurch BH23 13 E5
Victoria Rd,
Fordingbridge SP6 11 C3
Victoria Rd,
Lymington SO41 21 C3
Viking Cl,
Bournemouth BH6 12 A6
Viking Cl,
Southampton SO40 10 B5
Viking Way,
Bournemouth BH6 12 A6
Viking Way,
Christchurch BH23 13 G6
Villette Cl BH23 12 A1
Villiers Rd SO45 17 E6
Vimoutiers Ct SP6 11 E3
Vincent Cl BH25 22 B4
Vincent Rd BH25 22 B4
Vinegar Hill SO41 21 D3
Viney Rd SO45 19 F6
Violet La BH25 22 C3
Viscount Dr BH23 13 G4
Vitre Gdns SO41 19 E5
Vixen Walk BH25 22 C2
Vulcan Way BH23 13 G3

Wadmore Cl SO45 17 G2
Wagtail Dr BH25 22 A4
Wainsford Cl SO41 18 B4
Wainsford Ct SO41 18 C4
Wainsford Rd,
Everton SO41 24 B5
Wainsford Rd,
Lymington SO41 18 A5
Walhampton Hill SO41 19 F2
Walkers La North
SO45 10 A4
Walkers La South
SO45 10 A6
Walkford La BH25 15 G2
Walkford Rd BH23 15 F3
Walkford Way BH23 15 E3
Walnut Cl BH25 22 B4
Walnut Cl SO42 7 D3
Wanstead Cl BH24 25 D1
Warnes La BH24 8 B4
Warren Av BH23 13 F5
Warren Pk SO41 21 A1
Warren Pl SO40 26 C1
Warrys Cl SO45 17 F6
Warwick Av BH25 22 C4
Warwick Rd SO40 27 E3
Water La, Hythe SO45 16 D5
Water La,
Southampton SO40 26 C4
Waterford Cl SO41 19 F4
Waterford Gdns BH23 14 D5
Waterford La SO41 19 F4
Waterford Pl BH23 15 E5
Waterford Rd,
Christchurch BH23 15 E5
Waterford Rd,
New Milton BH25 22 D4
Waterloo Rd BH23 13 F4
Waterloo Way BH24 25 C4
Watermans La BH25 17 E6
Watermead BH23 12 A5
Watermill Rd BH23 12 A2
Waters Green Ct SO42 7 D3
Waters Grn SO41 7 D2
Watership Dr BH24 25 E4
Waterside,
Christchurch BH23 13 F6
Waterside,
Southampton SO45 17 F1
Waterside Cl BH24 25 C1

Waterside Sq*,
Waterside SO45 17 F1
Watery La BH23 13 F1
Watson Walk SO40 26 B5
Wavendon Av BH25 15 H4
Waverley Cl SP6 11 E2
Waverley Rd,
Fordingbridge SP6 11 E2
Waverley Rd,
New Milton BH25 23 C5
Wayside Cl SO41 21 D2
Wedgewood Gdns
BH23 6 D1
Well Cl BH25 23 A5
Wellands Rd SO43 20 C3
Wellers Cl SO40 26 A4
Wellesley Av BH23 13 H3
Wellington Av BH23 14 A5
Wellington Cl SO45 16 D5
Wellington Ct BH25 22 C3
Wellington Pl SO40 9 C2
Wendover Cl BH25 23 A6
Wenlock Ct*,
Hunt Rd BH23 13 F2
Wentwood Gdns
BH25 23 E5
Wessex Av BH25 23 B5
Wessex Cl SO45 10 A5
Wessex Est BH24 25 D2
Wessex Rd BH24 25 D2
Wessey Cl BH23 13 H3
West Cl,
Bournemouth BH6 12 A6
West Cl,
Lymington SO41 18 B4
West Common SO45 10 A6
West Hayes SO41 19 F3
West Hill Dr SO45 17 E2
West La SO41 24 B4
West Mills Rd SP6 11 E4
West Rd,
Christchurch BH23 6 B3
West Rd,
Lymington SO41 21 B2
West Rd,
Southampton SO45 16 D6
West St,
Fordingbridge SP6 11 E4
West St,
Ringwood BH24 25 A3
West St,
Southampton SO45 17 E2
West View Rd BH23 12 D4
West Way SO41 18 C5
Westbeams Rd SO41 6 C5
Westbury Cl,
Bransgore BH23 6 B3
Westbury Cl,
Christchurch BH23 14 A3
Westbury Cl,
New Milton BH25 23 C6
Westbury Rd BH24 25 D3
Westcliff Walk SO45 17 F1
Western Av BH25 15 H4
Western Rd SO41 18 D3
Westfield Gdns BH23 13 G1
Westfield Rd,
Lymington SO41 19 G4
Westfield Rd,
Southampton SO40 27 E4
Westgrove SP6 11 E3
Westlands BH23 6 B2
Westminster Cl BH23 23 A8
Westminster Rd SO41 21 B3
Westmoreland Ct
SO41 24 A2
Westover Rd,
Lymington SO41 21 D3
Westover Rd,
Southampton SO16 27 H3
Westwood Cl SO40 27 E1
Westwood Rd SO43 20 B2
Wetherby Cl SO40 26 C3
Wetherby Gdns SO40 26 C3
Wharncliffe Ct BH23 14 D5
Wharncliffe Gdns
BH23 14 D5
Wharncliffe Rd BH23 14 D5
Whartons Cl SO40 4 C2
Whartons La SO40 4 B2
Wheelers Walk SO45 10 A5

Whimbrel Ct BH23 13 F4
Whinfield Rd SO45 16 D6
Whitaker Cres SO41 18 C4
Whitby Cl SO41 21 C3
Whitby Rd SO41 21 B3
Whitcombe Cl SO40 26 D4
White Barn Cres SO41 24 B2
White Hart La SO40 9 B2
White Heather Ct
SO45 17 F1
White Horses BH25 23 A8
White Knights BH25 23 B8
White Lion Courtyard
BH24 25 A3
Whitecroft SO45 17 F4
Whitefield Rd BH25 22 B4
Whitehall BH23 12 B5
Whitehart Flds BH24 25 D2
Whitehayes Rd BH23 12 C1
Whitemoor Rd SO42 7 A3
Whites La SO45 10 D2
Whitewater Rise SO45 17 E5
Whitley Way BH25 22 C2
Whitsbury Rd SP6 11 D1
Whittington Cl SO45 17 E4
Wick 1 Ind Est BH25 22 A4
Wick 2 Ind Est BH25 15 H2
Wick Cl BH25 15 H2
Wick Dr BH25 23 A5
Wick La,
Bournemouth BH6 12 A5
Wick La,
Christchurch BH23 12 B5
Wick Point Mews
BH23 12 B5
Wickfield Av BH23 12 A5
Wickfield Cl BH23 12 B4
Wicklea Rd BH6 12 B6
Wickmeads Rd BH6 12 A6
Widbury Rd SO41 18 C5
Widden Cl SO41 6 C5
Wide Lane Cl SO42 7 C3
Widecombe Dr SO45 16 D3
Wildburn Cl SO40 26 B1
Wildcroft SO40 26 C5
Wildfell Cl BH23 12 A1
Wildground La SO45 17 F6
William Cl BH23 15 E2
William Ct BH23 15 E5
William Rd SO41 19 E2
Williams Ind Pk
BH25 15 H2
Willow Av SP6 11 E2
Willow Dr BH23 12 A5
Willow Pl BH23 12 B4
Willow Walk BH25 23 C8
Willow Way BH23 12 A5
Willowdene Cl BH25 22 D4
Wilton Gdns BH25 22 A4
Wiltshire Gdns BH23 6 A2
Wiltshire Rd BH23 6 A2
Wilverley Cl SO41 18 C5
Wilverley Pl SO45 10 A4
Wilverley Rd,
Brockenhurst SO42 7 C3
Wilverley Rd,
Christchurch BH23 13 F3
Winchester Rd BH25 22 D2
Winchester Way SO40 26 B5
Windermere Gdns
SO40 21 E4
Windmill Cl SO41 21 D3
Windmill Copse SO45 17 E5
Windrush Way SO45 17 F4
Windsor Cl SO41 24 A1
Windsor Ct BH23 15 E5
Wingate Rd SO40 26 D4
Wingfield Av BH23 14 B3
Wingrove Rd SO40 4 B2
Winsford Cl BH23 14 A3
Winsor La SO40 9 F1
Winsor Rd,
Cadnam SO40 9 D3
Winsor Rd,
Southampton SO40 27 F5
Winston Ct BH23 23 B6
Winston Ct*,
Stour Rd BH23 12 A3
Winston Way BH24 25 C2
Winton Cl SO41 19 G4
Winton Way BH25 22 C2

Wisbech Way SO41 24 B3
Wolfe Cl BH23 12 D3
Wolsey Way SO41 21 E3
Wood La,
Brockenhurst SO42 5 A2
Wood La,
Lymington SO41 21 D3
Wood Lawn Cl BH25 23 A6
Wood Lodge SO40 26 B2
Wood Rd SO40 4 B3
Woodcock La SO41 24 C2
Woodfield Gdns BH23 14 B3
Woodford Cl BH24 25 D3
Woodgreen Walk
SO40 26 B3
Woodhayes Av BH23 14 B3
Woodland Way,
Christchurch BH23 14 B5
Woodland Way,
Lymington SO41 21 C3
Woodlands Cl,
Christchurch BH23 6 B2
Woodlands Cl,
Southampton SO45 17 E6
Woodlands Ct SO45 17 E6
Woodlands Rd,
Brockenhurst SO42 7 C5
Woodlands Rd,
New Milton BH25 23 A8
Woodlands Rd,
Southampton SO40 4 A4
Woodlands Way BH25 22 C1
Woodley Gdns SO41 18 D2
Woodruff Cl BH23 13 H2
Woodside Av SO41 19 F5
Woodside Cl SO41 19 F5
Woodside Gdns SO40 4 B3
Woodside La SO41 19 E5
Woodstock La BH24 25 B3
Woodvale Gdns
BH25 22 D3
Woodville Rd SO45 10 C2
Worcester Pl SO41 19 F4
Worthy Rd BH25 22 B4
Wortley Rd BH23 14 D5
Wren Cl,
Christchurch BH23 13 G5
Wren Cl,
New Milton BH25 23 A5
Wren Cl,
Ringwood BH24 25 E4
Wychwood Dr SO45 10 A6
Wykeham Pl SO41 19 E4
Wyndham Cl BH23 15 F3
Wyndham Rd BH23 15 F2

Yaldhurst La SO41 18 B3
Yarrell Mead SO41 18 B3
Yarrow Cl BH23 13 H2
Yelverton Av SO45 17 F6
Yeoman Ind Pk
SO16 27 H2
Yeoman Pk SO16 27 H2
Yeomans Way SO40 27 E4
Yeovilton Cl SO41 24 B5
Yerville Gdns SO41 24 A2
Yew La BH23 22 D3
York Av BH25 22 C4
York Cl SO40 27 F3
York Pl BH25 22 C4